ILLNESS AND CRISIS | COPING THE JEWISH WAY

Rabbi Tsvi G. Schur

D1403453

Published by the National Conference of Synagogue Youth/Union
of Orthodox Jewish Congregations of America, 333 Seventh Avenue,
New York, NY 10001.

Distributed in Israel by Mesorah Mafitzim
J. Grossman, 117 Rechov Uziel, Jerusalem

We acknowledge with appreciation permission to quote from:

My Name is Asher Lev by Chaim Potok, © 1972,
    Alfred A. Knopf, Inc.

Aging, The Fulfillment of Life by Henri J. M. Nouwen and
    Walter J. Gaffney, © 1974, Doubleday & Company, Inc.

Good Grief by Granger E. Westberg, © 1962, Fortress Press.

We acknowledge with appreciation permission from Nancy Freiman
to print her personal article "A Jewish Response to Crisis."

ISBN 1-879016-07-9

Produced by Olivestone Print Communications, Inc.

Printed in the United States of America

This book is dedicated to these people, each of whom has made a marked impression on my life.

Rabbi Chaim Schmelczer, dean of the Chicago Telshe Yeshiva, my teacher during the beginning years of rabbinical school, whose kindness, concern and sensitivity for people made a lasting impression on me.

The late Dr. Raymond Ratnoff, a physician of New York and Miami Beach, who epitomized dedication and concern for his patients. He was a source of great pride to the medical profession.

My beloved family, my wife Malke, and my children, Esther Brocha, Betzalel Mordechai, and Basya Tehila, who have taught me, by their being, what gifts of God are.

A Publication

in the

JOSEPH TANENBAUM LIBRARY Series

ב״ה

Dear Rabbi Tzvi & Celia,

I have read your work on relating to occasions of sorrow in general, and sickness in particular, with great interest.

I believe that your readers will derive insight and benefits from their perusal.

Your approach and presentation are fully in accord with the traditions and wisdom of the Jewish faith.

Please accept my best wishes for Hashem Yisborach's blessing in all your undertakings and in the Divine wealth you are performing particularly.

With deep personal regard,

[signature]

Rabbi Yaakov Weinberg
Ner Israel Rabbinial College

RABBI AARON SOLOVEICHIK
PRESIDENT

I read the pamphlet entitled: "Illness and Crises, Coping the Jewish Way" very thoroughly twice and I found it beautiful, impressive and touching. The great French philosopher and writer, Pascal, wrote: "There is a logic of the heart just as there is a logic of the mind". Tzvi Schur's pamphlet on "Illness and Crises" is imbued with logic of the mind and logic of the heart. This pamphlet is of great value not only for Jewish Rabbis, Jewish Chaplains and Jewish doctors but also for gentile ministers, gentile chaplains and gentile doctors. The title: "Illness and Crises, Coping the Jewish Way" is also expressive and reflective of the human and humane way for the simple reason that the Jewish way and humane way are one and the same thing.

Rabbi Aaron Soloveichik
Rabbi Aaron Soloveichik

CONTENTS

ACKNOWLEDGMENTS

I extend my sincere appreciation to these individuals whose comments and critical evaluations helped make this book a reality: Fred Rosner, M.D., Director of Medicine at the Queens Hospital Center of Long Island, N.Y., Abraham Twerski, M.D., Chairman Department of Psychiatry, St. Francis Hospital, Pittsburgh, PA., Lawrence Hurwitz, M.D., Chief of Oncology, St. Joseph's Hospital, Milwaukee, Wisc., Donald Hay, M.D., Assistant Professor, Medical College of Wisconsin, Milwaukee, Wisc. I am honored that these individuals, each of whom has brought so much to his respective field, gave their valuable time to assist me in this work.

Sincerest gratitude goes to one of my most beloved and respected teachers, Rabbi Aaron Soloveichik, Dean of Yeshiva Brisk of Skokie, Ill. who, throughout my years in the Rabbinate and in my present field, has treated me not only as a student, but as a father would a son.

To the various rabbinical leaders of the Milwaukee Jewish Community, the reknowned scholar, Rabbi David Shapiro (may God grant him a complete and speedy recovery), Rabbi Michel Twerski, Rabbi Ronald Shapiro, and my other colleagues and friends for their assistance.

To the Milwaukee Jewish Federation, Mount Sinai Medical Center, Milwaukee Jewish Home, and other institutions that I have served for giving me the opportunity to be fulfilled in life by enabling me to help others.

To the late Rabbi Joseph Rothstein, former Senior Chaplain of the Jewish Chaplaincy Service, Philadelphia, PA., and Rabbi Abraham Pelberg, who originally introduced me to this magnanimous field of chaplaincy.

Personal thanks to Reverend Richard O'Donnell, Director of Pastoral Care, St. Joseph's Hospital, Milwaukee, Wisc., who opened my eyes to a new and sensitive world.

My deepest gratitude to Dr. Granger Westberg for writing a beautiful preface. Dr. Westberg's work as an author and as founder of the Wholistic Health Center depicts a concern for the total patient which we must all seek to emulate.

To my secretary, Audrey Wilde and my wife, Malke, for their typing skills and patience.

To my dear cousin, Dr. Irwin H. Goodman, to Dr. Barbara Gluck, and Gerald Glazer, who took time from their busy schedules to assist in editing this work.

Last but not least, to the thousands of people I have met in this field, be they colleague, hospital patient, nursing home resident or client. No matter what I may have added, and hope to continue to add to their lives, it can never be compared to what they have added to mine.

T.G.S.

PREFACE

Having been actively engaged in the field of pastoral care of the sick, first as a hospital chaplain, then as a teacher in medical schools, I have been waiting for a book like this one for a long, long time. And it is just what the doctor—or rabbi—ordered!

And it is just what I, as a minister, ordered! Along with thousands of other ministers, I have wanted to partake of the feast of Jewish tradition and literature which speaks so poignantly to the very questions which confront us in our day-to-day conversations with those who are ill. This book adds a deepening dimension as it assists us in wrestling with the mysteries of illness. We are grateful for the insights of distinguished religious sages of the past, many of whom we have never met before in our own literature.

Rabbi Schur, with his sensitive mind and heart, has dug deeply into his own soul and into the soul of the accumulated wisdom of his venerable heritage. We appreciate his sharing it with a wide audience. And he has presented it in a manner that is easy to read, easy to comprehend, and in many cases, easily applied to actual human situations of ministry.

A physician who read the manuscript voiced his appreciation of his interdisciplinary spirit of the author as well as his style and content when he wrote, "It was refreshing too, for once, to read a compassionate and understanding view of our (physicians') problems. You put into perspective the harsh, strident cries we usually hear about our profession and hold up a mirror for a more balanced appraisal of our situation in the world."

In similar vein, a rabbi responded to the manuscript in these words, "In my own ministry to the ill in the past twenty years, I have grappled with many, if not all, of the problem areas you address in your book and, not infrequently, have felt inadequate to the task. Your insights and anecdotes provide much food for thought, and I believe, will assist many of us in the helping professions focus more effectively on the problems we encounter."

It is my hope that many readers will be inspired by this book to continue the fine work that Rabbi Schur has begun—both as clinical practitioners of warm, loving care with a spiritual dimension and perhaps even as future authors who will expand upon the theme of this excellent book.

GRANGER E. WESTBERG, D.D.
Wholistic Health Centers, Inc.
Hinsdale, Illinois 60521

NOTE TO THE READER

This volume, based on many years of experience working as a clergyman in various hospitals, is an attempt to accomplish a number of goals. For the layman, it offers food for thought on those major areas of concern that we must all face: illness, old age and death. Here is a specific Jewish response to these universal problems. We sincerely believe that this response should have more than a passing interest for those of other religions as well.

Added to the bulk of the book is an appendix aimed more at the professional—the clergyman, doctor and nurse. Here is an examination of the different complementary functions of the health care team. Each must realize its interdependence with the others. Of special importance to clergymen reading this, is the author's clear call for more clergymen to enter this most difficult but fruitful work.

Although geared more to the professional, the layman who wishes to understand more of the personnel involved in the health care process will also find these pages invaluable.

TSVI G. SCHUR

INTRODUCTION

All of us are inevitably confronted by crises, regardless of our religious philosophies. Where we differ is in the attitude with which we face these crises. We may recall our first encounter with a crisis of illness or death through the loss of a loved one, or perhaps the loss of a pet. My own first encounter with the realization that life in this world does not go on forever, and that illness and crisis are realities of living, came when I was a young child watching television. I heard a news bulletin reporting the death of a prominent individual after a prolonged illness. As I recall, my initial reaction was fear; I realized then that this precious gift of life has many challenges.

Little did I dream then that, some thirty years later, I would be dealing with people facing these challenges and threats to life, and would be called upon to bring consolation and comfort to them.

Illness and death are powerful and frightening realities. As a trained hospital chaplain, I daily encounter people in varying degrees of crisis; from those suffering a simple fracture to others whose days are preciously few. To a person who uses his limbs professionally, a severe fracture can bring an immediate fear of what will happen next. Even though one must be able to overcome a handicap, learn to compensate, and discover new capacities, the individual is now facing, in his mind, a certain stage of death. An injured professional baseball player shared with me the first feelings he had when he felt his leg give way. At 25 years of age, he thought to himself, "What can I do now? What is there that life can offer to me now? My whole world is centered around sports." Fortunately, his injury healed and he returned to his profession; nevertheless his accident forced him to confront a stage of death.

In all degrees of illness, whether headache, common cold, flu, wounds, arthritis or more serious medical complications of the various cancers or heart disease, the eternal question asked at such times, is "Why?" Why need man suffer? Why tragedy? Why the snuffing out of a life of a child, teenager, or young adult? Why does aging and life in general mean facing a crisis for one person, while it is a time of beauty for another?

This book tries to confront these questions. It is not intended to be a book of Jewish Medical Law. It has been written for the benefit of every individual who is facing or has faced crisis—the patient, family, clergyman and medical professionals. Although it may possibly evoke sadness and pain, I hope it may also awaken an appreciation of what we have and a constant awareness that only through faith can we overcome the pains of life and enjoy the beauty and fulfillment it brings us.

The word *life* is probably the most mysterious and challenging word in our language. To most people, it is a beautiful gift, a wonderful experience, where even challenges and difficulties are seen as a time for beauty and fulfillment. To others, life is something from which one desires to escape. There are those whose sufferings and disappointments in life make them wish they were never born. Their bitterness often can be detected in their relationships with other people. Rather than accepting a helping hand or searching for understanding, these people may tend to take the coward's way out. A coward can attempt to hide, but the real hero seeks guidance, rolls with the punches and rises up again, smiles at joy and hopes for more, cries at sadness but longs for its end.

The greatest investment in the future is to keep trying, keep striving, avoid stopping and giving up the effort to stay alive, and to always resist the temptation to "cop out". In the final analysis, the will to live is the strongest force in the world. Pessimistic responses to life are mortal enemies, more to be feared than death itself, because they can produce in us a living death. Hope for the future is the vaccine that protects one from infections of pessimism and despondency.

The great Jewish sage, Rabbi Israel Meir Kagan, better known as the *Chofetz Chaim* (Seeker of Life), was noted for adhering to the beautiful Psalmic verse, "Who seeks life? One who loves the days and sees good therein" (Psalms 34:13). According to one interpretation, the emphasis in on seeing *good* therein.

In *Illness and Crisis: Coping the Jewish Way* I share intense human experiences with you. I do not claim to have all the answers, for some answers do not exist. I remember the story of a man who once came to the great Rabbi Mendel of Kotzk to pour out his bitter heart. He and his wife had many woes and they did not know where to turn. Rabbi Mendel listened intensely to him while keeping his eyes lowered. After a moment of deep meditation, Rabbi Mendel raised his head, looked straight into the man's eyes, and said, "I am not equal to the task of consoling you after such cruel suffering. Only the true Master of Mercy is equal to that. Turn to Him."

I, too, cannot hope to erase suffering and pain. I can only hope that, by sharing my experiences, I will at least have stimulated thought and brought some comfort and understanding to those who seek it.

WHAT IS PASTORAL COUNSELING?

Pastoral counseling is defined as a process in which the insights and principles of theology and the behavior sciences are used to develop the wholeness and health of individuals, couples, families, groups, and social systems. Professional pastoral counseling is a discipline, like other disciplines, such as clinical psychology or family medicine. The process is learned in doctoral level study beyond the basic graduate degree in theology or psychology. Pastoral counselors are members of the clergy, but clergy are not necessarily pastoral counselors. A pastoral counselor must be one who brings into his profession first and foremost human understanding and caring, coupled with theology, and for the Jewish pastor, true Torah philosophy. The pastoral counselor, as a therapist, is assumedly an expert, but if he is not first of all a human being, his expertise will be irrelevant and quite possibly, harmful.

We find ourselves living today in a world of searching. So many people feel unfulfilled and are desperately seeking some meaning and purpose to their life. While the clergyman was at one time viewed as primarily a pulpit occupant or strictly a teacher, today, more people seek him out as a friend; a person to turn to in time of need. Psychiatrists and psychologists, although they may be expertly trained in their profession, often lack a philosophical and religious background to this sensitive field of counseling. Physicians, unfortunately, are often too occupied with technical matters and not enough with the human being. Thus, the pastoral counselor's role, perhaps as a preface to seeing the psychiatrist, can bring a more complete solution to an individual's perplexing problems.

The pastoral counselor must view himself, in a sense, as a messenger of God, with a specific mission of emulating the attributes of the Almighty. As He is kind and understanding, so too, must we be kind and understanding. By the pastoral counselor's actions, by his listening and sharing, he can bring about a new bond between man and his Creator that could lead to a rebirth of ultimate happiness.

Whether it be in the synagogue or in the yeshiva day school, the rabbi or teacher must be a father image or, at times, a brother image; continuously showing his sincere concern about people. In today's society, where the break-up of familes is so prevalent, teachers and rabbis must restructure their roles to be the one person to whom, without any hesitation, an individual can feel free to turn at any time. Whatever the reason for the loss of present Jewish family values, the rabbi or pastoral counselor must deal with the results of social disorganization. Thus, the knowledge of counseling is a "must" for clergy today in order to be helpful to troubled people with social, emotional and religious concerns. At one time the clergyman was cautioned to relegate the responsibility of counseling to trained professionals due to his lack of knowledge and training. Today's demands by society make it imperative that clergy be aware of what the world of counseling entails.

While at one time rabbis would be called "religionists," today, they must be called "humanists." This, in truth, is the basis of the true "religionist." The Hebrew Theological College Jewish University of America is one of the few Yeshivos in the country today that offers a Doctorate in Pastoral Counseling, giving clergy an opportunity to gain new insights into the rewarding role of minister.

It is interesting to note that the word "pastor" is the Latinized form of the Hebrew word for shepherd. The King James version renders the Hebrew word "shepherds" as pastors in Jeremiah 2:8. Throughout the centuries the Jewish leader was compared to a shepherd. The Torah recalls Moses likening himself to a shepherd, with Israel as his flock. One of his most plaintive cries to God upon relinquishing leadership was the solicitude over the appointment of a successor so "the congregation of the Lord be not as sheep which have no shepherd" (Numbers 27:17). Just as God is the shepherd of Israel, so Israel's leaders must, in turn, care for His People.

Samuel was the outstanding counselor during the era of the judges. While traveling extensively he heard controversies, rendered judgments and reviewed adjudications. The Prophets were not counselors in the usual sense of the word, but one cannot read Jeremiah and Ezekiel without sensing that here were men of God who were particularly interested in things of the heart. It is not difficult to believe that these great men would have lent a sympathetic ear to those who came to them with burdens. They realized that people have problems because they are people. While today's rabbi must have some familiarity with clinical manifestations of mental illness in crisis situations, he must not forsake his own traditional resources and functions in extending loving concern, in sharing a religious orientation of life, a feeling of belonging, a power of faith, and a meaningful belief in God. It should not be said that clergy forget their religious background when they learn some of the basic skills of counseling. "True religion and true psychology," states the American Psychiatric Association, "are mutually enriching and should have nothing to fear from one another."

As a counselor, the rabbi must listen more than he speaks and empathize more than he judges. But what he does as a counselor is compatible with a total role he fulfills, both symbolically and actively. Hesitant to consult a psychotherapist, individuals often turn to the rabbi for comfort and reassurance. In such situations, the rabbi's role is a kind of first aid. He offers acceptance and understanding while helping an individual overcome his fears of seeking intensive therapy. The empathetic theme is especially strong in the teaching of the chassidim. They speak of "the descent" of the tzaddik, religious master. The master goes down to the level of the people, enters the pit in which they are sunk, experiences their fate as they live it and then rises with them. In order to keep from being lost in the pit with the sinner, the master binds a rope of faith around himself. He immerses himself in the situation of the other person, but is capable of extracting himself. Psychologically speaking, the tzaddik protects himself from over-identifying and maintains a link with his own separate identity. Many have categorized the Chassidic Rebbe as a humanistic psychotherapist who heals by instruction as well as through the type of relationship he extends to the Chassidic community. As Moshe Halevi Spero, in his outstanding work, *Judaism and Psychology: Halachic Perspectives* (p.111) writes, "to be sure, therapist and rebbe alike must be able to distinguish between true neurotic suffering and everyday misery. But in the modern view, both problems may rightfully constitute psychotherapeutic issues. The Kabbalistic goals of Yichud (unity), Deveikut (cleaving), and Hitlahavut (enthusiasm) are at once, psychological, interpersonal, and spiritual desiderata. To get well, is to be able to cope with loneliness, insecurity, doubt, mistrust, boredom, restlessness, and marital discord. These concerns of the modern psychotherapist were those of the Chassidic Master." While the Chassidic Master's relationship may essentially be religious, this does not detract from its therapeutic aspect.

It is told that the Kobriner Rebbe visited the Slonimer Rebbe and asked him, "Have your teachers left any writings as a heritage?" "Yes," replied the Slonimer. "Are they printed or are they still in manuscript?" asked the Kobriner. "Neither," replied the Slonimer. "They are inscribed in the hearts of their disciples." True Pastoral Counselors, understanding their complete role, can truly leave their message, not just by being teachers, through writings or sermons, but by their actions as individuals who have chosen an awesome field— a messenger of God bringing comfort in time of need.

I

THE PATIENT

I have noticed in my visits four types of patients. Each type will react to crisis in a different, sometimes unusual way.

The first type is the religious individual, who has a firm belief in God. The news of a serious illness is often taken as hard by this person as by anyone else, despite his belief. Even the believer is saddened and cries. Throughout history, we find instances where the greatest of saints did not want to die, not because they feared death, but because the religious, Torah-committed Jew understands this world to be one wherein we do our utmost to glorify the name of God, our Father and Creator. We perform *mitzvos* (good deeds), as we are taught in the book *Pirkei Avos* (Ethics of the Fathers— 1:3) "that we are to do them, not for the receiving of reward, but because of our love for God" and our love and appreciation of the gift of life that He has given us.

Hardly an individual can say that his whole life, every moment and every day, has been filled only with sadness. In all my interviews with patients, even those living with constant crises, I have found that when they are really honest with themselves, there is always a moment when they are thankful that they were given the opportunity to live.

The sincerely religious individual wants the opportunity to continue living. Death, to him, means receiving his reward, but this individual wants to "work" more, through heeding God's commandments, before he receives his final payment. His entire life is entwined with deep love, respect, and service of his Creator. When death calls, it is accepted more easily. The *Chofetz Chaim* is said to have taught, "It has

23

been observed that when we come into the world, we cry and the rest of the world laughs for joy. We must so live that when we leave the world, we can laugh while the rest of the world weeps."

A story is told that "when the hour arrived for Rabbi Simcha Bunam of Psyshcha to depart from the world, his wife stood by his bedside and wept bitterly. He said to her, "Be silent; why do you cry? My whole life was only that I might learn how to die." A similar story is told about Rabbi Israel Baal Shem Tov. As he lay dying, his disciples wept uncontrollably, "Why do you sob?", he asked them with a radiant, smiling visage: "I have been preparing for this moment all my life." On the other hand, the Talmud relates that King David tried to ward off death because of his desire to continue serving God. It is related that when the late renowned Jewish scholar and Torah leader, Rabbi Aaron Kotler, was ill, he asked some of his students to pray that he be given additional years, for he still had so much to accomplish.

The second category is that of the non-observant individual, who proudly associates with religion, but does not practice it. Yet, at the moment of crisis, he still recognizes that even the greatest doctor has limitations. When I, the chaplain, enter his room in a moment of crisis, he asks for prayer. He may even cry, displaying a moment of fear, regret, or perhaps guilt. Though he may be non-observant, the flickering flame of his belief is still burning.

The third category includes the agnostic, a person who is really not sure what life or belief is about. He too fears; although confused about his beliefs, he is not too reticent to call out for help. The agnostic, *when properly approached* at the right moment, may find comfort and even possible fulfillment in religion.

I am reminded of a case. Entering the room of a certain patient who was suffering from a terminal disease, I sensed his feeling of uncertainty regarding my visit. The patient told me that he had no need for a chaplain. I explained that, as a hospital chaplain, I visited all Jewish patients just to wish them well. In further talk he asked me what my Jewish philosophy was—Orthodox, Conservative, or Reform. I replied that I was Jewish. Detecting a smile, I told the patient that my visits are not intended to evoke a feeling of discomfort because of differences in religious philosophies. I continued to inquire how he was feeling. He responded by offering me a chair and asking me if perhaps I could help him find some comfort in facing his particular illness. He told me that he had a weak religious upbringing and suddenly now realized how much he regretted his lack of Jewish knowledge. He discussed his uncertainties concerning God with me, but felt with certainty that there was some master plan for man and for the world. When he asked, "Why is there suffering?" I answered by recalling a moving story related by Chaim Potok in his novel, *My Name is Asher Lev*. A young artist was reflecting about his introduction to death:

And I drew, too, the way my father once looked at a bird lying on its side against the curb near our house. It was Shabbos and we were on our way back from the synagogue.

"Is it dead, Papa?" I was six and could not bring myself to look at it.

"Yes," I heard him say in a sad and distant way.

"Why did it die?"

"Everything that lives must die."

"Everything?"

"Yes."

"You, too, Papa? And Mama."

"Yes."

"And me?"

"Yes," he said. Then he added in Yiddish, "But may it be only after you live a long and good life, my Asher." I couldn't grasp it. I forced myself to look at the bird. Everything alive would one day be as still as that bird?

"Why?" I asked.

"That's the way the Ribbono Shel Olom (God) made His world, Asher."

"Why?"

"So life would be precious, Asher. Something that is yours forever is never precious."

I noticed tears beginning to flow down this individual's cheek. I held his hand as he sobbed and asked me if I would say a prayer for him. (When a person asks me to pray for him or her, I always agree to do so but request that he or she offer a prayer on behalf of my family as well, for I firmly believe that my being a rabbi makes me no greater in the eyes of God than the individual who requested the prayer.) Before I left, I told him that my personal Jewish philosophy was Orthodox, for, in it, I found strong attachment to the Almighty and I found challenges easier to cope with. He asked if I would return. I did many times afterwards until his death. When he was semicomatose I entered his room and told him that it was the rabbi coming to visit. I asked if he would like to say a prayer with me. He nodded yes and together we recited the *Shema Yisroel* (the affirmation in the belief of God). Here was a patient who a few months before had been very confused and full of questions. He died with a sense of fulfillment and peace.

The last category is that of the self-proclaimed atheist, one who has completely denied the existence of God. The truly atheistic patient is extremely rare. I remember my late grandfather, Rabbi Abraham Schur, telling me of an incident in which he met a *claimed* atheist. During casual discussion with my grandfather he responded, "Oh, my God!" Though the atheist claims this was only a figure of speech, my grandfather observed, that even in the atheist a spark of belief, or at least of searching, exists subconsciously.

I have also found what I refer to as the *hysterical atheist*, one who has gone through suffering, denying God out of anger and bitterness. I recall a visit to a patient who, as she cried out her woes, told me that she had become an atheist and could no longer believe in God. I listened and then asked her, "OK, fine, but tell me, now that you don't believe, do you feel better? Has this eased your pain?" The patient was silent for a moment, then bursting out in tears, stated that perhaps she was just angry. If we turn away and say, "I don't need you, God," what have we really gained? In the long run, our true comfort comes from our Creator. As confused and angry as we may be, we must try to understand that God's ways cannot just be defined as a magic worker. By saying, "God, because you did this to me, I will never worship again, I will never give to charity again," do we believe that this will make God weaker? I believe that it will only make man weaker. God does not really need man or books to defend His actions. It becomes very dangerous to ourselves when we attempt to bring God to our level of understanding. We must realize that the human being and God lead two different existences. Though we seek to emulate God's attributes, we cannot think for one moment that our intelligence and knowledge is the same as His.

Atheism may arise not so much from bitter tragedies or challenges in life, but often from the lack of proper education. Although some consider every atheist a heretic, perhaps even to the extreme that he should be ignored, we must realize that he is a human being, and our obligation must be to deal with and care for him in his time of need.

Some have observed that the most sorrowful moment for an atheist is when he wants to plead for something or give thanks but does not know how or to whom.

Whether a patient is an atheist, agnostic, observant or nonobservant, he will still most often go through various stages of denial and bargaining. It is difficult for one to accept that he is ill and will have limitations, and not be able to accomplish all of the goals that he had set out to reach. Many patients will cry out to God, "Why me?", displaying anger. The observant may possibly regard his crisis as a punishment or a test of God. Others may feel that God let them down, or that God, perhaps, is displaying His anger at them for a reason that only they themselves may know.

Some patients, in the midst of the bargaining stage, will try to make a deal with God. "If I get well, I promise that I will give charity, I will do more for my synagogue, I will be a better Jew and thus a better person." I recall cases where people, while seriously ill, bargained with God and when cured, did in fact fulfill their promises.

CASE 1

Twenty five years ago a young teacher was critically ill. His family asked a famous righteous rabbinic scholar to pray for their loved one. In addition to giving charity, they asked his advice for other things they could do. The revered rabbi suggested that if the young man would accept upon himself to fulfill one additional mitzva (commandment) fervently, perhaps God would have mercy and rescind the decree. The teacher agreed, if cured, to dance and bring great joy to the bride and groom at every Jewish wedding. To this day, this teacher, who had been so seriously ill, is known for the unique excitement he adds to every wedding. His bargain with God was not taken lightly and was fulfilled.

CASE 2

A man, not particularly religiously observant, was suddenly stricken with a serious illness. During his coma, his wife asked a rabbi to request a renowned rabbinical leader to pray in her husband's behalf. Advice was given that the family should consider changing its way of life and practice the precepts of its religion more diligently. New tefilin (phylacteries) were purchased. A promise to observe the Shabbos day with intensity and a commitment to uphold Family Purity Laws was made. Miraculously the patient recovered. The family, true to its word, has become more observant, and has not forgotten God's kindness.

Unfortunately, I have also seen patients, who in the midst of critical illness, bargain with God, and yet when cured, forget all their promises and thus, in a sense, reneged on their side of the deal.

CASE 1

Mr. A. was rushed to a hospital for emergency surgery. Two days later, while visiting him, he said, "Rabbi, if I come through this illness, I promise that I will be at services in synagogue every day." The patient did recover, but never was seen in synagogue. Living not too far from him, I decided to pay him a visit. It was over a month after his illness and I told him that he was missed at services, which, while he was ill, he had promised to attend. Mr. A. began to give me various excuses, each of which had little validity. His wife, hearing my conversation, said, "I am sorry, but my husband really has no religious incentive." After further general discussion, I wished him well and left telling him that perhaps someday he would surprise me.

CASE 2

Suddenly a member of Mr. B.'s family had been taken seriously ill. At first, doctors gave little hope for the patient's recovery. Medical tests subsequently revealed a blood clot to the brain. Arrangements were made to fly the patient to a famous medical center for immediate treatment. Before their journey a rabbi happened to enter the intensive care unit area, and gave Mr. B. a sum of money with the instructions that upon his return it be given to charity. (Jewish belief is that if one is on the way to do a good deed, the person is protected from harm. By giving Mr. B. the money for charity, the rabbi made him the messenger for such a good deed—in this case, the giving of charity.) Mr. B. told the rabbi, "If this patient survives, I promise you I will make good on the money." With God's help, this patient miraculously survived delicate neurosurgery and returned to a full active life. As of this writing, at least as far as I am aware, Mr. B. has forgotten to make good on the charity donation.

As chaplain, I must realize that the patient, regardless of his belief, is a child of God, as well as a person in pain, and I must relate to him, not only on the religious level but as a fellow human being. Being a truly religious person of any denomination means being humane. Being humane means loving every person, be he of the same religious persuasion as yours, or of another faith. Our obligation as fellow creations of God is not to judge, but to love. The late great Rabbi Abraham Kook, former Chief Rabbi of Israel, when accused of being too friendly with heretics, said, "I would rather be guilty of undeserved love than of undeserved hatred."

In Judaism, the Talmud demands that we always pursue what is best for the patient. If the patient is a baby or child, he may not be able to express his feelings. Nevertheless, during illness, the child is undergoing a trauma. Therefore, even the smallest child, when ill, needs constant love and security.

Even if one suspects that the patient is unaware of his situation, either through coma or senility, one must attempt to communicate to him that someone who cares is there. A patient recovering from a stroke shared with me his personal traumatic experience. When the rescue squad arrived at his home, he heard the attendant telling his wife, "It seems that Henry has had a stroke." The patient related to me that upon hearing this he was petrified. Here he lay helpless not able to move or speak. He told me that he only wished the attendant would have been sensitive to the fact that a stroke patient can hear. He could have said, "Henry, we believe you've had a stroke but you will be okay." No words of comfort were offered to him. Jewish law states that out of respect to the deceased, a dead person must never be left alone (*Shulchan Aruch, Yoreh De'ah* 339:4)—how much more so then when one is alive, but ill?

One must recognize that the patient often fears the unknown, while the family fears the immediate crisis. We must be sensitive and thus aware that the fear of the unknown, as it pertains to the illness and its consequences, can be a much greater trauma for the patient than the fears that the family may have. We must, at the same time, never underestimate the family's anguish.

I remember most vividly when my first child was born. She weighed only two pounds and needed immediate surgery. Understandably, I was quite shaken. Here I was, a human being being tested by God. My parents had come from out of town to be with us, and I remember seeing tears in my father's eyes. I asked him, "Why are you crying even more than I, father?" And he answered, "My pain is as great or even greater than yours, because I see not only your child suffering but mine as well." The challenges that confront a family when one of its members is ill do not only involve immediate relatives, but affect every member of the family, and even friends.

Patients and their families react differently to pain and fear. I recall visiting an elderly female patient whom I had known for some time. She had had surgery for stomach cancer. While visiting, I asked how she was feeling and she said, "The night before I went into surgery, I was very worried and found it difficult to sleep." But then she told me that she said to herself, "Almighty, if it is destined that I should have more years—wonderful, but, if not, thank You so much for all You have given me."

Another patient who underwent mastectomy surgery shared a poem that she had read in the newspaper with me, and asked that I share it with others. She felt that this poem gave her tremendous strength and wanted others to benefit from it as well.

The room smells of roses and Russell Stovers.
Some foreign arm has been taped to my shoulder.
The nurses make no sound. (Polyester doesn't rustle.)
The Metropolitan Opera did 'Faust' for me today on radio. Demerol did the staging. I wish you could have seen it!
When I open my indolent eyes, the people who love me are searching my face to see how they should feel.

All the words I can say are so old, so used, so familiar. How I would love to be brilliant!

As soon as I know anything, I know that I am fine - this is not a catastrophe - it's only an inconvenience.

If this is a master plan to make me realize how many people love me, I do.

If this is a grand design to elicit promises of preserving my health, I will.

If there is no plan to this at all, I'm making it so.

I'm planning to work and play better.

I'm planning to appreciate the people who make me feel good about myself.

I'm planning to savor splendid moments and put hurts in the far corners of my mind.

Inhale your acrimonious tears; I'm planning not to need them.

A mastectomy or breast biopsy can be not only a physical fright for a female patient, but a psychological one as well. Besides fearing for her life, she also feels for her family and at times fears what her husband will think of her physically. There are patients who have gone through mastectomies with great fear, while others have shown a beautiful, positive attitude, despite their fear. The latter have shown a special determination not to let their crisis get the best of them.

Though many patients show a very positive attitude to their illnesses, there may come a time when families and patients say, "Let the agony end." There are times when the patient himself says to me, "Rabbi, please let God take me." As if I have the power! Yet I believe that even that patient (and any patient) in the moment of his greatest pain has a desire *not* to die, if he can somehow be relieved of his pain. He is willing to try any medication in order to be cured and live. For, in the final analysis, he feels life is worth living.

When there are differences between the family and the patient the family must realize despite their own feelings, they cannot impose their feelings on the patient. In *certain* instances we must be sensitive to what the patient is saying and thus allow him/her to make his/her own decision. I recall a specific example.

An elderly gentleman who had a history of heart disease needed immediate gall bladder surgery. The doctors feared that if the surgery was not performed, peritonitis would set in, and thus the patient would die. I was asked by the physicians to try to convince the gentleman to have the surgery, for he had been refusing to do so. The patient felt, at eighty some years of age, why take a chance on such surgery, especially since the risk existed that his heart would give way. Understanding the patient's rational fear, I consulted a rabbinical authority who felt that one could not force this patient into surgery, especially since the risk of heart failure was a reality. Though this patient's family wanted him to have the surgery, I explained to them that this choice had to be made, not by the physicians or family, but by the patient himself. Later the patient acceded to his family's request and had successful surgery.

When visiting elderly patients, I often hear responses of "I have lived a long life; it is time to return home." They seem to want to die rather than face the further challenge of old age. I jokingly tell them, "God has a whole world in His hands to worry about. He doesn't need you also at this moment." I have found that the "humor approach", when used properly, can really change the mood of a depressed patient.

Yet, we must sincerely acknowledge that death for the elderly, is at times, a welcome gift. To have lived a long and fulfilling life, and then to struggle through the challenges of an illness can be an extremely difficult task. When entering an elderly patient's room I may say, "May God be with you and bless you with good health." I have found patients often responding, "Rabbi, for what?" Then I answer, "Because you are a parent, you have children, grandchildren, and friends who consider you dear, you have a definite purpose for which to live." I will never forget one elderly woman who answered me so sharply, "Rabbi, parents are only parents when they can do something, when they have health, but when they are sick they become a burden."

Many patients of all ages voice feelings of depression and some even explicitly discuss suicide. Jewish law can never accept suicide, for it makes man the master of his own soul. We all belong to God. Thus, we have no right to destroy His creation by our own hand. An individual who contemplates suicide must bear in mind the agony that he can cause so many loved ones. It may seem an easy escape from an immediate crisis, but it will create future crises for other family members. Nevertheless, a patient who has these feelings of suicide, or any feeling of severe depression, must feel free at all times to discuss openly his fears and ideas with a chaplain, clergyman, or member of the medical care team. When even the slightest ray of hope exists, a person must never give up.

Recently, an individual with whom I had been close for some time shared with me the fact that she was going to take her life on a certain day. It was all planned and finalized. She decided to share this information with me simply because a cousin of hers had taken her life some time earlier and not shared her agony, her frustration in life with her. She was hurt that her cousin did not confide in her and reach out to her for some type of shoulder to lean on for friendship, caring and assistance. Being that I was such a help to her over these years, she did not want to hurt me the same way her cousin had hurt her. This individual was a very rational person and therefore my concerns were very positive and serious. I called her parents and shared with them the fact that, as Chaplain, I had been close with their daughter for some time and she had shared with me many of her frustrations, and now she was planning to take her life. Her father was shocked; her mother broke down in tears and said, "You know, Rabbi, we've seen a change in our daughter's personality; we've seen her unhappy, but for some reason we seemed to ignore it and just accepted it as a mood that she was going through. When you bring this to our attention of her plans to take her life, I begin to realize in fact how insensitive we have been and the tremendous lack of communication that has existed." Ultimately, the family went to the daughter's apartment, confronted her with the information I had given them; initially she denied it, but then broke out in tears, telling her parents and family that life just wasn't worth living for her any more. There was a lot of sharing, a lot of communication, parents telling a child how much they really cared and the child opening up and telling the parents what was hurting her. Simple, obvious things had not been communicated, had been covered up, because of fear of communication.

A week later I received a card from this distraught individual, who wrote to me the following: "At first, I was so angry that you indirectly prolonged my agony. On the other hand, I found out that my family truly loves me and cares about my problems. In essence, what I want you to realize is that my life has been deeply enriched by you, Sir, and I am so thankful that I have such a caring and beautiful person in my life."

Tragically, we live in a society today that deals with machines, computers, rather than people. We are forgetting to communicate, we are forgetting to reach out, we are forgetting to care, we are breaching the foundation of our Torah teachings—v'ahavta l'reacha kamocha—that one should love his friend as he does himself. We are becoming sadly, unintentionally perhaps, self-centered, concerned only about ourselves, and we are forgetting that we are all in this world together as brothers and sisters, as children of a Supreme Being.

Every person, every patient, is a sensitive individual. Interaction with him and meeting his needs must be governed by respect and concern for his sensitivities.

II

PARENTS IN CRISIS

Probably the most difficult moment for a family is to accept the death of a child, whether it be the sudden death syndrome or a long term illness. We expect parents to die, but not children. When parents are confronted with the crisis of a terminally ill child, it is only natural for them to cry bitterly and feel anger and pain, and ask, "Why is this happening to us?" We always hope that a cure for our child's disease will be just around the corner, but unfortunately it is not always so. We must treat the terminally ill child with special love, but, at the same time, not make him feel different from other children. Even children who are terminally ill are aware that they are going through a mysterious crisis. They may begin to ask "Why?" A parent must reassure the child that our Creator, in His mercy, loves us all and has some reason, though unknown to us, for putting us through these crises. Sharing these experiences and fears with family and close friends helps bring strength to one another.

The Midrashic story of Rabbi Meir may be difficult to simply accept. Nevertheless, in a pensive moment a parent suffering such a loss can recognize the depth of this story. Rabbi Meir, the great sage of the second century, had two beautiful sons. One Sabbath day, while the rabbi was teaching in the academy, the boys suddenly died. Beruriah, their mother, carried them to her room and covered them. In the evening when Rabbi Meir returned he asked, "Where are the children? I missed them at the study hall." Before replying, Beruriah handed him a goblet of wine for the *Havdalah* Service, which marks the conclusion of the Sabbath. She then set the evening meal before him. When he was through with the recitation of the grace after the meal, he again asked for the boys. "They are not far off," she again replied. And then she said to him, "Meir, I would like to ask you a question. Some time ago, two precious jewels were entrusted to my care. I cared for them to the best of my ability. I became very fond of them and felt as though they were all mine. Now the owner wants them back. Should I return them?" "I am surprised that my learned and wise wife should ask such a question," Rabbi Meir replied. "Of course the jewels must be returned to the owner." She then led him to the room and lifted the sheet which covered the bodies of their children. "Ah, my sons, my sons," the rabbi lamented. Whereupon his wife reminded him that they must return to the owner that which was entrusted to them. Together they recited the verse of Job which a Jew repeats at the death of a near one: "The Lord gave, and the Lord hath taken away. Blessed be the name of the Lord." Even Rabbi Meir, the great believer, cried; but he understood a child's life is a gift.

The Almighty's love for the soul that has been returned to its Creator is eternal. The Talmud states (Avodah Zarah 3b) that a child who dies is taught Torah at the footsteps of the Almighty. This may offer some consolation to parents who are firm in their religious beliefs and who acknowledges that a child is a gift of God, but the pain remains for them as well as for all other parents.

I have often asked parents who have suffered the loss of a child whether had they a choice, would they have wanted this child for as many years as they were blessed with him, or not have had the child at all? The answer has almost always been that, despite the great loss, they were appreciative of the gift of years they had.

I know of couples, childless for many years, who have asked me to help them find a child to adopt, even if the child was slightly handicapped, for all they seek is the opportunity to share their love in a family environment.

I will never forget the incident of parents who came to a Chassidic rabbi for comfort and interpretation, after their child was born blind. The rabbi told them that "One must understand that God has created various souls, all holy in nature. At times these souls are placed in physical bodies that may be imperfect, thereby needing a special kind of love. God has chosen your family to have this child and cherish this soul." Although it is a traumatic experience and sometimes even tragic, if a person sincerely loves and has a deep belief in his Creator, he will cherish God's gifts despite the great emotional and financial demands.

One of the greatest challenges to parenthood is the mentally handicapped child, whether due to Down's syndrome or brain damage developed at birth or due to later illness. Having taught retarded children for a year, I can attest that the one thing they most definitely respond to is love. I read with interest the view of a mother of a retarded child, who served as a volunteer member of the National Association for Retarded Children for many years. She wrote, "Though we as parents of retarded children are faced with a multitude of problems, many unanswerable questions and a great deal of grief, yet we do have our compensations . . . One of the favorite themes that permeates my conversations is how much our children have meant to us. This thought runs like a bright golden thread through the dark tapestry of sorrow. We learn so much from our children; retarded children are wonderful teachers if we are not too proud to learn from them, and the grief of parents leaves little room for pride. We learn so much in patience, in humility, in gratitude for other blessings we had accepted before as a matter of course; so much in tolerance; so much in faith—believing and trusting where we cannot see; so much in compassion for our fellowman; and yes, even so much in wisdom about the eternal values of life because deep agony of spirit is the one thing which can turn us from the superficialities of life to those things that really matter. We also gain much in developing a strange kind of courage which enables us to face life without cringing because, in one sense, we have borne the ultimate that life has to offer in sorrow and pain.

"Where, in all of this wide, wide world could we go to

learn such lessons as these lessons dealing with the real meaning of life? Where else could we ever learn so much from those who know so little?

An illustration of this is given by Dr. Richard C. Woolfson in a recent article in the *Journal of Jewish Communal Service* (Spring 1985, Vol. 61, no. 3). In certain ways, he writes, the Judaic outlook is that the mentally retarded child should command even deeper respect than the child with normal faculties. On one occasion the Chazon Ish (1879–1954), a great Jewish Torah leader of the 20th century, surprised everyone by standing up to greet a mentally retarded child. He explained this act of respect by stating that an individual is placed in the physical world by God, in order to correct himself; to perfect himself, and he does so by following the *mitzvot*. Yet, because intelligent choice and intention are needed to fulfill a *mitzva*, a mentally retarded person generally cannot perform a valid *mitzva* (though there are some exceptions.) The Chazon Ish reasoned that since everybody is to strive for higher spiritual achievements, and since the mentally retarded do not have this means of self correction, then this must mean that the souls of such people are already pure. Therefore, he stood up in the presence of a mentally retarded child as a mark of respect for a soul which was so pure it did not need further correction.

It is understandable that not every family can cope with this tremendous challenge. Many retarded children are placed in government institutions, but a parent must not cut off the link of love and concern.

One of the most tragic experiences a parent can face is the loss of a child by a criminal act or an accident. I remember being called to console parents whose daughter's life had been snuffed out at the hand of a criminal. They were extremely bitter against God until we reached a moment of insight, when I explained that we must refrain from blaming God for man's inhumanity. If anything, this was the time to turn to Him, for only in God and religion can we hope to find any solace.

The father told me how hard it was for him to recite the

Kaddish (prayer for the deceased) and praise God after this tragedy. I tried to explain to him my personal concept of what *Kaddish* is really about. By saying *Kaddish*, we are showing the Almighty the tremendous influence that the beloved deceased had upon us. When she is judged, the Almighty can say, "Look what this child accomplished. She left her family with that much love and devotion, that even in a moment of deep grief and sorrow, they stand before Me and sing My praises." I explained how truly precious was this life in the eyes of God, and that there was no question that she would receive the ultimate reward that is in store for all of us after this life. The father later told me that his saying *Kaddish* was no longer a challenge but had become a moment of comfort.

A sudden miscarriage can be a shocking blow to a family waiting for that special little cry. Although a miscarriage is usually a medical sign that the body has discarded something unhealthy, a loss is still felt. When a woman knows she is pregnant, she begins to order her life around the baby. She had a promise of the future, and now this all has come to a sudden end. A woman who had suffered a miscarriage cried out, "Just because no child was born and just because I didn't feel the life of that baby doesn't mean I didn't love, lose or mourn its leaving! So many people seemed to think I didn't REALLY lose anything. Well those people make my baby a non-person! It wasn't a paperweight or a rock in my uterus. It was MY BABY—someone—even if I never saw the color of hair or shape of face—a baby was there, just the same!" During a hospital visit I was called by a sobbing woman, who had just suffered a miscarriage in the sixth month. She told me that she realized it was for the best, but how could she control her feelings when she had carried life within her? She asked me, "What is going to be done with the fetus?" I, in turn, replied with a question by asking her what she wanted done with it. She asked whether according to Jewish law it can be buried, for she felt that the earth marked, in a sense, the return home of this potential Godly gift. In traditional law, I explained, the majority of authorities state that burial was not only proper, but required. I told her that I would take care of her request. After I notified her that the fetus was buried, I noticed a sudden change, a psychological relaxation.

After the miscarriage, many things may remind the mother of her loss: leaving the hospital empty handed; seeing babies, mothers, and women who are pregnant; playgrounds, parks and maternity stores; packing away maternity clothes; baby product commercials on TV; anything. Most of the time both fathers and mothers feel they are in some way to blame for the miscarriage. We are a people who are taught to be in control, to be responsible. When something goes wrong we are taught to re-examine what we could have done or should have done to change the outcome. We feel there "must have been something" we could have done. It is therefore so necessary for our sensitivities to be so special, and to recognize the extent of grief of both parents and family in crisis.

As an observant Jew, I believe without a doubt that there is a Godly reason for every single thing that happens in this world, from a sudden crib death to the agony of a patient in pain. A child's death is most traumatic, but unfortunately we forget that life itself does not guarantee longevity.

The Torah-oriented Jew firmly believes that, from the moment of birth, the length of one's life is predestined. At times, through our own negligence, we alter this plan. If one consumes too much alcohol, drives while intoxicated, and consequently is killed in a car accident, the act of becoming intoxicated is one that has been controlled by man's free will. At any time after birth, we are old enough to die. Nowhere is it written that man *must* live seventy or eighty years; one person can accomplish in thirty years what many cannot accomplish in seventy. A child in infancy can bring the gift of love that many in seventy years cannot.

If we, as humans, are to become complete, life will send us not what we want, but what we need in order to grow. Life will confront us with many demands. As psychologist Carl Jung wrote: "Life always tries to produce an impossible situation to force the individual to bring out the very best.

Becoming whole does not mean being perfect, but being complete. It does not necessarily always mean happiness, but it does mean growth. It is often painful, but fortunately, it is never boring. It may not be getting out of life what we think we want, but it is the development and purification of the soul."

In the final analysis, we must acknowledge that life is a gift, but it is not completely ours. From the moment we are born, the time seems to tick away until life comes to an end. We must cherish and appreciate this gift, especially when with our loved ones.

It is unfortunate that we take for granted so many of God's gifts. It is amazing how our attitudes and priorities can change overnight. Facing illness or crisis with our loved ones, the luxuries of life, such as new furniture, a new wardrobe, or a special trip suddenly become very unimportant. At that moment we decide that our main goal should be to enjoy all the beautiful things we have: our children and parents, our families and friends. I recall vividly a teacher who reprimanded our class for wasting time; he noted that a moment wasted can never be recovered. While we have it, we must appreciate time and use it to its fullest.

Only through trust and faith in a Supreme Being can we begin to come to terms with our crises. In our blessing for each new month we ask that God should fulfill the requests of our hearts "for good." The interpretation of the phrase "for good" is that only God knows what is best for us, since man is usually blind to what is truly good for him.

Readers may question my ability to write about the loss of a child. Besides having my first child born ill (though thank God she is healthy today), and then losing a three day old child, I have also experienced the emotional pain of miscarriage together with my wife. So I can understand the pain of one who suffers these difficult crises of life.

My mother-in-law, stricken with leukemia, passed away at a very young age. I have shared the grief of members of my family who lost their loved ones, both children and adults in the Holocaust. I have watched dear friends die, I have watched fellow human beings suffer, and I have shared that suffering. Despite all, because of my deep faith, respect, and acceptance of a Deity, I firmly believe that for all of us who face crisis, life goes on; and in the midst of the darkest cloud we can also see a ray of sunshine.

Man has been given a special gift, the ability to accept. This does not mean wiping out the crises and the memories, for the scars remain; but it does enable us to continue living.

To those readers who have lost a child, I recommend *The Bereaved Parent* by Harriet Sarneff Schiff. It is a true story of a family who lost a child and managed to cope. *The Soul of the Matter* by the gifted scholar and author, Gershon Winkler, shares Jewish teachings worth reading. Many families who have read these sources have come to better cope with their loss. I hope they will bring comfort to you as they did to me.

III

NURSING HOMES AND THE SENIOR CITIZEN

We live in a society that accepts sending parents to nursing homes. Often we hear parents complain about the way their teenage children treat them. I wonder if these parents ever reflect on the way they may be treating *their* parents.

I am sensitive to the potential conflict created when a parent lives with adult children. It is true that there comes a time when children have to live their own private lives; does this mean the neglect of parents? Throughout the Torah, throughout Jewish learning, we are taught to respect our elders. We read in Leviticus (19:32), "You shall rise before the aged and show deference to the old." Though the Jewish people basically can be proud of the example they set for society of respect for elders, there are still many who forget that the aged are the ones who have given our lives meaning, that they are the ones with the experience and the knowledge.

Many refer incorrectly and insensitively to nursing homes as "old age homes", which only aggravates the challenging problems of growing old, and evokes a deep and threatening fear of the future. We live in a society where enough fears of aging exist. People spend literally billions of dollars to ward off old age, whether it be with face lifts, hair coloring, or through other medical or cosmetic means. Gray hair or a wrinkle are no longer accepted as harbingers of the aging process. Unfortunately aging has become an experience with which today's society cannot deal comfortably.

Everyone wants to live a long life, a life which is happy, interesting and rewarding. But one has to grow old to do it, and one must want to live, no matter what happens. For many of America's millions of citizens who live past 65, the trouble (unfortunately) hardly seems worth it. But those of us who have experienced a Torah-education upbringing know how Torah greats, though old in years, are young in spirit because they never consider themselves old or useless. They feel needed, and they *are* needed; and they will be forever. For others, aging is a time of anguish, loneliness, sadness, and sometimes poverty. These problems are common for those senior citizens who find themselves in nursing homes.

A nursing home must exemplify its name: a place of nursing for an elderly person who is in need of care, and, at the same time, a home, where that person continues to feel wanted. A nursing home must never be a place for children to rid themselves of a problem.

How sad is my feeling when visiting people in nursing homes, only to learn that the children have not visited or called in weeks, or even for months. How suspicious I feel when I hear someone say with a sense of satisfaction that his parents live in Florida. Yet, when visiting many of these residences in Florida, we sometimes find that they are unfit for anyone in which to live. Sending parents to Florida to retire and then forgetting them while children live their own lives, is hardly any way for anyone to be fulfilled. To this day I shudder when I think of two incidents during my chaplaincy when visiting nursing homes.

CASE 1

I entered the room of an elderly man and found him weeping. He had been living with his children until his son decided to place him in a nursing home, and then did so as if he were delivering a package. I took the initiative of calling the son and was told that his wife gave him a ultimatum—either her or his father. I told the son that though I was sensitive to his problem, perhaps he should seek counseling to correct the situation and not simply strip his father of any self-respect or deny him the respect due him.

CASE 2

A resident in Florida had taken ill. The children who lived out of town were called and informed of the situation. The social worker recommended that the daughter fly in. Later I learned that the daughter stated that she was just too busy and would be unable to make the trip for another few weeks.

Though these instances are fortunately not common, the fact that they exist is enough reason for concern.

Before placing a parent in a nursing home, many families go through a great deal of trauma and difficulty. In this chapter, I cannot answer clearly whether children should keep parents in their home or send them to a nursing home, because each situation must be evaluated individually. One fact, though is clear. At times, nursing home care can be a sign of respect for parents. When a parent is placed in a home but visited or phoned regularly, the parent has not been cut out of his family. If anything, the child who placed the parent in the nursing home has performed a great *mitzva* (commandment) in honoring his parent, for he is paying for care that might not be available at home. At the same time, he can offer his parent the ability to live in the midst of peer friendships and peer security.

Before placing a parent in a nursing home, children should make a thorough investigation; part of the *mitzva* of respect. They should ascertain that the nursing home is not just a money-making concern, but a place where the accent is on bringing happiness and fulfillment to the remaining years that a beloved one may have. A good nursing home has many programs that bring out the creativity in its senior citizens, and thus enables them to continue to contribute to life. I have seen nursing homes that have outstanding activity departments. Many hidden talents in art, tapestry, music and writing have been discovered by the residents.

I feel pity for the child who has made the decision to place his mother in a nursing home and then forgets her, for he may consequently suffer severe guilt. One should realize, when placing an elderly parent in a nursing home, that many adjustments are required of the parent, and unfortunately many times children do not understand this. Children may blame the nursing home for their parents' discontent. Yet, this may be their own displaced guilt feelings. There are times when children try to do too much for their parents, not realizing that they are unconsciously stripping away their parents' self-respect. Psychiatrists and social workers have told me that often when children bring a senior citizen for counseling it is not the parent who needs the counseling, but the children.

Entering the nursing home may signify to the parent that this is, in a sense, the last stop. Sometimes, those who must enter homes for the elderly have to sign over to the home all their possessions. Although many elderly have acquired, through hard work, enough money for their retirement years, they still tend to feel less dignified when they can no longer earn their own living or control their finances. Many nursing homes have their own banking facilities, enabling residents to maintain financial self-respect. I remember how my beloved grandfather, who was in a nursing home, had the custom of always giving us a gift before the holidays. He would go to the nursing home bank and give us the gift, and thus felt that he had not been stripped of any self-esteem.

The parent may feel cut off from the family; this may be caused by the family's failure to visit or call. A child must realize that after entry into a nursing home, the parent, who for years was the master of his own home, is no longer ruler of his castle. If an individual hospitalized for the first time has fears, so much greater can be the fears of a parent entering a new environment in a nursing home.

In the nursing home a senior citizen may go through

periods of isolation and aloneness. Isolation is a physical state, a geographic position. One can be surrounded by people and yet be alone. A patient in a nursing home is usually not isolated, but aloneness is an intensely experienced feeling. Thus, we must interact with the senior citizen to overcome this feeling of being alone.

Viewing the senior citizen, we often see what we call hallucination, whereby the elderly person creates a world of his own, perhaps reliving the past or talking about things that never occurred. Why is it that when a child does similar things it is perceived to be imagination, yet in an elderly person it is considered to be senility?

Many times children underestimate their parents. Parents in their aging years are much more clever and keen than we think. I have noticed, for example, then when tragedy strikes, children try to protect their parents. Yet, parents are often better able to cope with tragedy than their children. When I hear families say that their elderly parents don't recognize them anymore because they always confuse their names, I wonder; "Don't we all sometimes call our children by the wrong names?"

Serving as chaplain in a Philadelphia hospital, I entered the room of an elderly patient and was told by the family that their father was completely incoherent. Yet, as I neared the bed, the patient immediately recognized me as the rabbi, and called me closer to his bedside. In another incident, the children told me that their father was incoherent and near the final stages of life. As I approached his bed, I said to the patient, who had been a member of my synagogue for many years, "I don't know if you can hear me, but if you can, would you like to say the *Shema Yisroel* together with me?" Not receiving a response I continued, "I will say the *Shema*, and you repeat after me if you can." To the amazement of his family the man recited almost half of the *Shema* with me before he passed on.

In my visitations with senior citizens I have observed with interest that those who have lived their lives surrounded by the companionship of books and a thirst for knowledge are less likely to become lonely and lost, for the search for knowledge can be everlasting. I have also observed that the religious senior citizen copes much better with his own aging. The importance of "religious feeling" was clearly recognized by Jung, who stated, "Among all my patients in the second half of life, there has not been one whose problem in the last resort, was not finding a religious outlook on life. It is safe to say that every one of them fell ill because he had lost touch with that which the living religions have given to their followers, and none of them have really been healed who did not regain his religious outlook on life.

On one occasion I walked into the room of an individual and identified myself as the rabbi. The patient looked at me and asked, "A rabbi? Why, I haven't seen a rabbi in over 50 years", whereupon he began to sob heavily. I moved closer to him and asked, "Why haven't you seen a rabbi in so long a time?" He responded, "Because I married a *shikse* (a gentile woman)." I asked him whether his 50 years of marriage were, in fact, good years. "Yes," he answered, "they were wonderful years, but I wouldn't recommend it to anyone." I wondered why, seeing that he had been happy. "Because now that I am about to die," he answered, "what do I have left of my Jewishness? It all ends now. My children are not Jewish; I have nothing Jewish left over. The memory and life of my parents whom I loved very much—despite their objections to my marriage—all ends because I did not perpetuate my religion." I left the room moved, very shaken, that here was a dying man, who, despite the fact that he had been happily married for over 50 years, now realized that his life was not complete, because he had abandoned his faith.

Senior citizens need security in the midst of a health crisis, despite their advantage of experience in living. Once, while I was visiting a retired doctor who was very ill, he looked at me and asked, "Rabbi, I dedicated my whole life to helping my fellow man. Why do I have to suffer like this?" Of course I had no answer, but I became aware of the fact that an older person, especially one who served as a doctor, must never be considered retired, or hear himself described in the past tense. People who have been helped by a doctor are eternally grateful, their appreciation never ends. News of the physician's illness can be a blow to the thousands of patients who had turned to him in moments of need.

Even though the retired physician becomes ill, and may be justifiably depressed and frustrated, he must never forget and we must never let him forget what he has contributed and always contributes to mankind, because he has scored high in the ranks of life. We forever cherish his wisdon and guidance.

For these reasons, it is up to us to see that individuals who are older in years, wherever they may be, maintain the respect and dignity that is incumbent upon us to give them, and that they most certainly deserve.

Children must be sensitive to all their elderly parents' needs. It is their obligation to ascertain that placing their parents in a nursing home will not compromise the religious lifestyles of their parents. Even if children are not strict in their own religious observance, they have no right to deny that of their parents. Too often, I have seen parents who adhered to the laws of kashrut all their lives placed in non-kosher nursing homes for the children's convenience. Children must see to it that if a parent is placed in a nursing home, it be one with the best care, and that they never neglect their obligations of the fifth Biblical commandment, that of honoring one's parents.

I am elated when people tell me that they visit or volunteer their time at nursing homes, because I understand the joy that they bring to the residents. "Numerous students spend most of their four year college education almost exclusively with their peers, unable to play with a child, work with a teenager, talk with an adult, or have any human contact with the elderly." Many times I have heard the deans of rabbinical schools, including one of my own "Roshei Yeshiva", Rabbi Jacob Ruderman of Ner Israel in Baltimore, discussing the importance of older students being concerned with the younger ones. "Those who are separated in order to be educated find themselves at times in a situation in which the educating contact of life is taken away from them. Being in close contact with peers during the formative years is extremely valuable and important, but when there is no world around you as a reminder of where you come from and where you will go, that closeness might lead to stagnation instead of mobilization, and that is a real tragedy."

It is also important to listen. What an individual can learn from an older person is endless. I marvel at the sharpness of the minds of many people well into their 80's. There is listening and there is *listening*. Try *listening*—really *listening*; it can enrich your life. *Listening* is the art of both seeing and hearing. The eyes perceive the nonverbal body language; the ears hear the words. Imagine a baby seeing and hearing, as he watches and listens to every move and every word of his parents. Likewise, we adults can *listen* with both eyes and ears. Listening builds a bridge between people; one strengthens the other. When our great teacher, *Moshe Rabenu* (Moses) spoke to the Children of Israel, he instructed "that the elders should be asked, and let them enlighten you" (Deuteronomy 32:7).

I recall a rabbinical student who would come to my grandfather and would sit down and listen with great thirst to his tales of European Jewry. I observed how my revered grandfather loved to relate these episodes of his lifetime, and also how this young rabbinical student sat there absorbing every word of knowledge; the bridge of communication was solidly built.

When the elderly can no longer bring us into contact with our own aging, when we have delusions of being ageless and immortal, then not only will the wisdom of the elderly remain hidden from us, but the elderly themselves will lose their own deep understanding of life. For who can remain a teacher when there are no students willing to learn?

Love learning and enjoy its fruits all your life, for this will help destroy loneliness, inadequacies, and fears. Our *mussar seforim* (ethical treatises) continuously exhort us to live each and every day that we are blessed with life to our maximum capacity, for each day can be an exciting chapter in the story of the rest of our lives.

A SPECIAL PROBLEM

A particularly sensitive problem is that of younger patients sticken with a debilitating disease or injury that confines them to life in a nursing home. Most often this decision to place the child in a professional care environment is made after a sincere attempt by the family to care for the child at home. The great expense and personal sacrifice demanded by this kind of care frequently creates other complex problems within a marriage or a family. These problems can destroy the basic support systems that are so desperately needed in any familial environment.

When such a decision is to be made I urge families to seek guidance in helping them deal with their decision. As with nursing homes for senior citizens, every effort must be made to find and choose a reputable professional care environment with dedicated and caring personnel. At times, this may even mean placing a loved one in an institution many miles from home.

Though this is an emotional and trying time, the family must not be concerned with what "people might say." As long as the family remains involved in some way, through occasional visitations or other suggested means of care, there is no reason to feel guilt or any sense of abandonment. Though guilt is a natural feeling, parents must not blame themselves for this misfortune in their life. They must view it as a challenge and meet the test.

People must understand that *institutionalization* (read: "appropriate residential placement") *is more often a positive alternative and not giving up or failure.* A family going through this traumatic period must be able to feel comfortable in reaching out to family and friends for support and understanding, as they now attempt to put their lives into a different perspective.

IV

THE DOCTOR AND THE HEALTH TEAM

The Torah teaches (Exodus 21:19) that a doctor is a servant of God, and that it is sinful for one who is ill to refuse to see a doctor (Talmud Bavli, Bava Kama 46b).

Most doctors realize that they are only messengers of God, able to provide and accomplish only a limited amount. When an oncologist told a woman whose husband had surgery that cancer had been found and his future was bleak, the woman begged the doctor to do everything possible to heal him, for her husband was her whole life. The doctor answered compassionately, "I can only do so much. I work for Someone much greater who makes the final decisions in human life."

It troubles me when I counsel families who are in sudden shock over the loss of a loved one because the physician had "given" the individual two years to live and he only lived two months. If doctors would use the powerful words *"I just don't know"* more often, it would give real meaning to this statement.

I have met physicians who believe sincerely in God and who are very active religiously, and those who have no belief at all. I asked a religiously oriented doctor, "How is it that some doctors do not believe in a Greater Force?" He replied, "Rabbi, I can ask the same question. How can someone who continues to see the trauma of illness, and at the same time, miraculous recoveries, not believe in a Supreme Being?"

Unfortunately there are doctors who have witnessed what they themselves refer to as "miracles", yet for some reason find themselves far from religious beliefs. It is interesting that in the various specialties of medicine, feelings of religion range from non-existent to strong. I have observed that most doctors who are actually involved with patients on a daily basis do believe in a Supreme Being, while many whose medical practice emphasizes a scientific approach, such as research or academics, feel that there is no room for spirituality. These doctors feel that, with enough experimentation there is no need for God, for science will eventually uncover all the hidden mysteries of life.

When dealing with patients, many of the non-believing physicians feel that they must maintain strong objectivity (which was, according to many, Freud's philosophy), but they do not realize that by being completely objective, they also, in a sense, may become dehumanized. Whether a doctor believes in God or not, by taking his oath as a physician, he has dedicated himself to healing mankind. Although I, as a religious individual, would only be treated by a doctor who acknowledges that his powers are limited, most patients are primarily concerned with a doctor's abilities rather than his philosophies.

I feel that patients and families sometimes fail to appreciate the work of the medical profession. It is true that there is a minority of doctors whose financial concerns are too great. But why focus on the tiny minority when the majority of these men and women are deeply dedicated to their chosen field?

I have watched residents on the floors of hospitals during cardiac emergencies banging on the chest of an older person (who some say has already lived a long life), in an effort to save him. This doctor's mission is to save a human life. I have seen doctors and nurses, their hands bloodied, working hours on end caring for a patient, and not for a moment worrying about themselves, even unconsciously neglecting their families because of their dedication to healing. The family of a physician or nurse gives up much by sharing their husband, father, wife or mother with so many in need. These families can be proud, but patients sometimes fail to realize that these medical professionals have families who need them too.

I have witnessed doctors who are described by patients as unemotional, showing deep emotion in private because they were frustrated in a medical mission.

Patients, families, and the medical field have every right to expect a doctor to be sensitive to the complete needs of the patient; the doctor is not just treating a disease, but a complete human being, emotionally as well as physically. Thus, a physician, in meeting the total needs of his patient must be aware of the patient's occasional apprehension in seeking a second opinion. Unfortunately, too many patients fear that such a request will offend their doctor. It is incumbent on the physician to make the patient feel comfortable, perhaps by making the suggestion himself. *A physician seeking consultation to confirm a diagnosis in no way diminishes his capabilities as a competent physician; it enhances his role as a dedicated and concerned professional.*

I have also (though rarely) encountered situations in which a patient has been diagnosed as incurable and asked for controversial medical treatment that may differ with the medical philosophy of his physican. If a doctor has come to the final conclusion that nothing else can be done to save the patient's life, he should be sensitive to the request of his patient, despite his personal objection, and permit the treatment in question, as long as it will not cause further damage or hasten death.

The health care team must always be aware that life's stresses, as well as ethnic background, can cause a patient's or his family's irritability.

Jewish patients and their families who have survived the Nazi camps may, in their moments of crisis, relive all their fears and past tribulations. There are times when medication given to such a patient may cause a hallucination that the doctor or nurse is his enemy and he must fight back to survive.

"The Jewish mother syndrome" is one in which the very nature of our living has placed the mother in the domineering role of queen of her household. She is mother, teacher, doctor, cook and thus there is a difficult adjustment when she or a member of her family is placed in another's care.

Sensitivity to the difference between *caring for* a patient and *taking care of* a patient meets these human needs. One can *take care of* an object, but we *care for* a living being.

There are times when a doctor is detached or impatient, but we must realize that the physician is preoccupied with many stresses; physicians are as fallible as laymen in the face of continuous crisis. Physicians as well as nurses go through days, weeks, and months working to save lives, and sometimes meet with tremendous frustrations that may disrupt their own emotional feelings; a crisis that they too must acknowledge and attempt to resolve.

Most physicians don't let their egos get out of control; they realize that their victories or cures are not their own, but must be shared with their Creator. When a physician loses his sensitivity because of a "mightier than thou" attitude and can no longer relate to people, it may be time for this professional to reevaluate his attitude and for the patient to find a new doctor.

I asked a renowned cardiac surgeon, a man who deals constantly with life and death situations, if he could describe his feelings about coping with the constant pressures he faced. In sincere humility he told me that he would not be human if he had no emotional reaction, but he felt as a professional in his field, that he deserved no thanks for the talents with which he has been gifted, because this is expected of him. But, I have witnessed, after this surgeon had saved lives that others had given up, his difficulty in facing the patients' family. I saw how families would want to hug and kiss him, while he unconsciously withdrew from sharing in their emotional expressions. I strongly feel that it would mean so much if any physician in a similar situation would simply say to a grateful family, "I'm glad I was able to help." Similarly, in moments of loss, it is not professionally demeaning for a physician to say, "I'm sorry," or even to shed a tear with the family. Physicians should be aware that although the patient is their primary concern, the patient's family must not be neglected. Especially when caring for a child, the medical team must be constantly aware of the family's emotions and concerns.

A legitimate controversy is whether a critically ill patient should be told that he may die. One side argues that nothing be hidden from the patient, thereby enabling him to "put his house in order." The other group argues that this notification may so depress the patient that he will lose all determination, will and fight to live. I have come to learn that most seriously ill people sense what we think are secrets. I do not necessarily feel that a young person without a family must be informed that his illness may be terminal. If we are confronted by the patient with the question, "Am I going to die?", we must always instill hope, and at the same time acknowledge with sincerity that although things at present may not look encouraging, our Creator has the final word. This, among other sensitive issues, should be discussed openly between family, physician and clergyman.

The physician and medical team must accept the fact that the clergyman and chaplain play a crucial role in the welfare of their patients. The help that the clergy or chaplain provides to the medical team can be invaluable. In times of crisis, patients often feel more comfortable confiding in their clergyman than their physician. Doctors must also be aware that patients often ask a clergyman familiar with the medical field about a specific physician. Though clergy are not medical authorities, they do have the right to share their recommendations and feelings when asked.

Besides the nurses, the clergy are the ones who visit the patient most often, and are able to sense feelings of fear and anxiety that the patient may have. In my role, I have given doctors information of which they had been completely unaware, and by doing so, helped their treatment of the patient. It is imperative that more physicians call upon the chaplains and clergy to help a family cope with a medical crisis. Doctors should be sensitive to the fact that though the patient initially anticipates their arrival and would prefer to see the doctor rather than a member of the clergy when the two visits coincide, the doctor should politely imply that he would like to examine the patient. Without question, the clergyman should relinquish his time, realizing that not only does the patient await his doctor's visit, but the doctor, himself, is usually on a very tight schedule. However, when a person is hospitalized, more time should be spent by the physician to give emotional support to the patient. Time spent at the office can usually be limited. Similarly, the doctor should be aware that there are times when a chaplain may be very engrossed in an important discussion with the patient, offering spiritual healing. The doctor's visit can hinder what the chaplain is accomplishing. While visiting a patient who was emotionally distraught, tearful and opening up to me, a doctor suddenly interrupted. Seeing the situation, he could have said he would return. To be a team and meet the complete needs of the patient, we must work with and respect each other.

Jewish law states that anyone who has the ability to save a life, and does not do so, is guilty of shedding blood (Shulchan Aruch, Yoreh Deah 336:1). When a human being needs basic medical assistance, it is imperative, by all laws of humanity and decency, that physicians must try to save the person's life. As doctors and servants of God, they have one obligation, and that is to attempt to save lives. I shudder when I read of hospitals that turn away patients without justification. Those families who have created a fear of malpractice lawsuits against the medical profession, also add to the potential disaster of other patients not being treated. They too must then share in the guilt of man's inhumanity towards man.

Patients and families must always feel free to speak to their physician about any problem. I have recently noticed signs in medical offices that state, "I invite you to discuss frankly with me any question regarding my services or my fees. The best medical service is based on a friendly mutual understanding between doctor and patient." I urge patients to accept this sincere invitation extended by your physician. It is in this manner that the doctor can achieve total fulfillment, and the patient, most often, ultimate security.

Let us appreciate all those who have dedicated their lives to the world of medicine, realizing that it is because of them, God's gift to us, that the majority of illnesses are cured and life is sustained.

V

HOSPITAL CHAPLAIN AND CLERGYMAN

More than 40 percent of people seeking help turn first to ministers. Often the clergy is a more acceptable source of potential help than the psychologist or psychiatrist, who may be viewed by many as a doctor who treats "crazy people." It is vital, therefore, that members of the clergy understand their own strengths and limitations and their role in serving the patient. In dealing with the patient, clergyman, chaplain, doctor, and nurses are all equally part of a health care team, all serving the patient by meeting different needs. The Book of *Avos* (1:6) states that "one should make for himself a teacher, a rabbi, and obtain a friend." This does not necessarily have to be two separate individuals. By making for oneself a teacher, by turning to a clergyman, one is automatically acquiring for himself a friend; someone who cares and who has dedicated his life to helping those in need.

Entering the hospital room, I, as a chaplain, must evaluate the patient's needs, either in a spiritual sense, or just in the vein of friendship. The chaplain or clergyman is not designated by God to pass judgment. We chaplains must never play God; just as the physicians are the Almighty's workers, we must remember that we are His servants as well.

A chaplain must never come into the room of a patient (especially a stranger) and dictate religious philosophies. If a parent acts as a dictator toward his child, he will either drive the child away or create further psychological problems for him. This will also occur if the clergyman is not sensitive to his relationship with the patient. We must enable our patients to feel our concern and love. A chaplain wrote that when we, the clergy, visit, we must ask ourselves, "Do I feel that the dialogue that I have just shared helped me to deal with my pain both physically and emotionally? Would I, as 'patient' want me, as 'rabbi' to come back?"

Clergymen should show the family that they are coming as concerned friends. Not always do we as clergymen have to enter into dialogue. There are times when our silent presence is all that is needed. The patient and the family should see that those who have chosen to serve God in a special way are people with whom they can be comfortable. In this way, when the patient becomes well, there will be a greater opportunity to bring the patient and family closer to understanding the beauty of his religion, and give his life new meaning.

An understanding and sensitive clergyman can provide invaluable assistance to families in working through doubts, conflicts, and feelings of loss, and in drawing on their resources of faith for strength and purpose. An individual in the midst of terrible pain is not interested in hearing assertions that all will be well. He is too engrossed in his pain to be rational.

Jewish law states that one is not to comfort the mourner when the dead lies before him. "Dead" does not have to be interpreted literally; crises are also in the realm of the "dead lying before him." In the moment of crisis, all the patient or family needs is to realize that someone is sensitive to what they are going through. Hospitals are becoming more aware of this need, and thus they are developing more complete chaplaincy and pastoral care programs to help the patient and family during these trying moments.

Patients and family must realize that the visit of a clergyman does not mean that death is imminent. The *mitzva* of *bikkur cholim* (visiting the ill), is a continuous display of human caring. The family must also accept the right of the patient to decide whether or not to have clergy visitors. It troubles me when I consider the attitudes of different families. Some families will specifically request that I visit their loved one, yet others (unfortunately due to lack of knowledge) fear that my visit may frighten the patient. Some patients call to see me, yet when I enter the room among family visitors, they act as if they had never requested my visit. Yet, in a private moment they confide that they didn't want their children to worry. How sad it is that a rabbi, or chaplain, or any clergyman has to symbolize fear rather than friendship. Perhaps the clergyman may be guilty of this perception if he only makes himself available during crisis situations. The lay person must remember that a good rabbi is first and foremost a human being whose care is unending. A true spiritual leader is interested in all facets of the life of his parishoners and fellow Jews.

Parents, sometimes, try to protect children in many other situations. I came into the hospital room of a young adult, and his mother refused to allow me to visit. What was the fear? From what was she protecting her child? There comes a time when a person, especially a young adult, must grow on his own. Parents who protect their children from the visit of a clergyman, fail, in a sense, to bring completeness to their child.

It hurts me when I enter a sleeping patient's room, and before I can leave, members of the family jump up and ask me not to awaken the patient. When someone has just returned from surgery, I have received a similar response. Does the family really believe that the clergyman is so insensitive he cannot realize when a patient is to be left alone?

Precautions should be exercised when visiting the psychiatric patient, unless the clergyman is well trained in mental health care. One comment from a clergyman who is not familiar with a particular patient's problem can cause a great setback for the patient and for those professionals working on the case. When I am asked by a psychiatric patient or his family to make a visit, I will first review his case with the physician involved so as not to interfere with the treatment.

I have heard families accusing clergymen of not visiting the sick, but in the majority of these cases, the families have failed to inform the clergyman that the person was ill. A clergyman who intentionally does not visit the sick, for any reason, should review his duty in his role as a servant of God.

It is sometimes difficult to visit a patient with whom one is very close. But when is the need greater? I personally have cried with patient and family. It is not shameful for a man to cry. This is part of the sharing experience; it does not mean failure in counseling, it means understanding and sharing in grief. The human being has been given tear glands; if the Almighty did not want us to cry or grieve, we would not have been given emotion or tears. Expressing our emotions through tears, or even at times through anger, helps us to cope with crisis.

Both clergymen and lay people tell me that nursing home visits present their greatest personal challenges. Can it be that those individuals are repressing their own fears of someday being a nursing home resident? Perhaps it may be their indignant feelings of the whole concept of a nursing home, yet they must not deprive these residents of that which they can bring by means of a visitation. If a clergyman (or any other individual) has a problem in knowing how to react to a particular situation, there is no shame in seeking counseling from a specialist in the field.

I have found that a clergyman's or chaplain's visit is appreciated beyond words by the great majority of patients. By visiting, we find great fulfillment as human beings and give added meaning to the title "clergy."

There are various ways of relating to patients. The body is the instrument for the giving and receiving of love. People isolated by serious illness have the same needs as others. The lonely aged are often best comforted by a smile or holding of hand, or touching of face. As a student in the day school or yeshiva, I remember how much a rabbi's simple gesture of pinching me on the cheek meant to me. I felt that the teacher cared, knew that I existed, and considered me important.

We, as clergymen and chaplains, realize that there is a time to live and a time to die. There is a time to smile and a time to cry. There is a time to give meaning to life and fight for what it means. There is also a time to be silent and to serve, not in the role of clergyman, but as human being, which is in itself a magnanimous role.

I cannot ignore the fear that many families have of clergymen. Yet, many times, this stems from their own guilt. We as clergymen must not fear bringing out the guilt of our people, lest we fail in our religious duties. There must be a time and a place for everthing. I urge synagogue clergymen to attend lectures at the various hopsitals which will give them an insight to a new world, which is, in truth, part of pulpit responsibility. *Mere ordination does not prepare one for the sensitive mission of helping others, or ourselves, deal with the crises of life.*

I cannot deny, that in my role as chaplain, I too go through periods of depression and helplessness, as I am sure do many of my colleagues who only deal with the ill. Often I have been emotionally shaken after visiting with a patient. When entering the room of a terminal patient, or of one who has gone through a great trauma, I have been confronted with many challenging remarks, such as, "Rabbi, I am going to die!" My reply is usually, that "I, too, am going to die." Though the patient may look at me in surprise, we must all realize that no one has any guarantees, for the next moment or day. It is to these patients who express their fears, that we can bring special comfort by just being there.

Despite these depressing moments, when a patient or family expresses their gratitude to you, and finds comfort in your visit, you are rededicated to your responsibilities.

In conclusion, I would like to share with you this most beautiful and meaningful poem that I saw on the wall of a hospital corridor. I am confident that it will give you the strength to bring added fulfillment to your *Avodas Hakodesh* (your holy work).

AT DAY'S END
by John Hale

Is anybody happier because you passed his way?
Does anyone remember that you spoke to him today?
The day is almost over and its toiling time is
　　through
Is there anyone to utter now a kindly word of you?
Can you say tonight, in parting with the day
　　that's slipping fast
That you helped a single person of the many
　　that you passed?
Is a single heart rejoicing over what you
　　did or said?
Does the man whose hopes were fading now with
　　courage look ahead?
Did you waste the day or lose it?
Was it well or sorely spent?
Did you leave a trail of kindness or a trail of
　　discontent?
As you close your eyes in slumber, do you think that
　　God will say, "You have earned one more tomorrow by
　　the work you did today"?

VI

THE VISITOR

Visiting with one who is ill (*bikur cholim*) is one of the greatest *mitzvos* (good deeds) a person can do. The Talmud states (Nedarim 39) that there is no limit to the *mitzva* of visiting the sick. The Talmud also teaches (*ibid.*, 40a), quoting Rabbi Akiva, that whoever does not visit the ill, is as though he has committed murder. Why such a strong statement by this great scholar and saint?

Visiting patients, I have come to understand the beauty and truth of these words. The visitor, entering the room of a patient who has been diagnosed as incurable, experiences a fear of "What do I say?" In many instances the person would rather avoid making the visit. For example, when one hears that a patient has cancer, the term seems to be too powerful a concept to cope with. We visit the patient as if he is dying, when in fact many cancers are now curable.

We, as the visitors, whether we be clergyman, chaplain, family member or friend, must ask ourselves when a beloved one or friend is ill, "Why are we so concerned about *our* feelings? Aren't we being selfish? How would we want to be treated in a similar situation?" I do not deny that these reactions are normal and realize that one must cope with his own feelings. Too often, though, *too* much self-concern is the problem.

How disturbed I was when visiting a woman who had had a mastectomy to learn that she feared her husband would no longer find her attractive or would lose his affection for her. I assured her that her husband did not love her any less. She responded with tears, saying that her husband had not been in to visit her for two days. Though I thought of the emotional pain her husband must be going through privately, I left her room thinking, "What more important time is there to conquer our own feelings, as difficult as that may be, and concern ourselves with another's?"

Rabbi Akiva's teachings deal with this subject. Whoever does not visit the ill lends, in fact, to an individual's suffering, because the ill person who is already depressed, now also feels unwanted and lonely. If his friends are not there in time of need, then what meaning does life have for this patient? It is a psychologically proven fact that if a person does not want to live and loses all will to do so, he begins to refuse treatment, does not eat properly, and thus hastens death. Is it possible that the friend or family member, by not visiting, is contributing even to a minute extent to the individual's death?

When visiting a sick person we must recognize that it is the *patient* who is physically and often psychologically suffering. No chaplain, friend, or family member can feel the *same* pain that the patient himself feels. The visitor might share the understanding of pain with the patient, but can never honestly say, "I feel exactly what you feel." The book of *Avos* (2:4) states, "Do not judge your friend until you come to his place." My father, Rabbi Daniel Schur, analyzed this statement and interpreted it to mean that we can never judge our friend because we can never actually reach or be in his place, for the moment that he moves it is no longer "his place." No two people can stand in exactly the same "place" at the same time. Specialists in grief counseling have emphasized the fact that no two people are alike. A family is a collection of individuals. When a crisis occurs in a family it occurs to individuals.

We can grow more if we are concerned about others. We must always be concerned about the life experiences and feelings of others; we should see that they are treated as we would want to be in a similar situation. Visiting a patient is not the time to relate one's own problems. The visitor must be aware who, in fact, is in need of visitation. The visitor must leave the patient with encouragement and not with further worries.

When visiting a stranger, one should never enter the room without being prepared for conversation. Patients have related incidents to me where a visitor would introduce himself and then sit and look in silence, lost for words. The visitor should first either try to find out something about the patient, or upon entering the room pick up on something. Many flowers and cards usually mean many friends. A picture of a child next to the bed can be another way of introducing conversation. Books in the room, or even perhaps the TV program being watched can also lead to a discussion. These few minutes of proper visitation can take a patient away from his thoughts of depression and bring a little joy both to himself and the visitor as well.

Visitors and families must also be sensitive to the realization that illness and crisis can alter the personalities of people. Medication and pain can cause someone to unintentionally offend a friend or beloved family member. Words said under severe stress should not be taken to heart, realizing that this is usually just a release of frustration and fears.

When making visitations there are times, though very few, when a patient will nervously or harshly ask a visitor to leave. When this happens to me, I softly express my good wishes and leave, realizing that there are moments when the patient must work through his/her own anger.

Jewish law states (Shulchan Aruch, Yoreh Deah 193:1) if there exists an ongoing disagreement between two people, one should not visit the other when he is sick, for such a visit may disrupt the patient's healing process. If a person wants to bring about a reconciliation, family members should be spoken to first to get permission from the patient for such a visitation.

In the process of recovery one must have will, desire, and fight. Those who visit patients make their battles easier to win, for there is no limit to the psycho-social and spiritual support that a family or visitor can contribute to the individual confronted with illness.

I share with you two specific cases.

CASE 1

A mother of four was scheduled for open heart surgery. I had visited her a number of times. All but one of her children lived out of town. I asked whether any of them would be coming to be with her and her husband. She said that her children had their own lives and she sincerely did not want to impose on them to come. I detected no bitterness, but a sincere feeling of a mother not wanting to bother her children. As the day of surgery neared, the patient became quieter and displayed a great amount of emotion and fear. The day before surgery, while visiting with her, I saw she was quite down. As I walked out of her room, I saw her children coming down the hall. They came in to be with their mother and father. When this woman saw her children, it was like a light had been turned on in a dark room. As tears flowed down her face, I, too, could not help but be overcome by the scene. The day of surgery came and the patient went into surgery with normal fears, but also with a determination that with God's help she would make it, and she did.

CASE 2

An elderly lady in a nursing home had been quite depressed. However, once when I came to visit her, she seemed like a completely new person. She shared with me that her granddaughter had just had a baby and that she would come with the child in a few weeks to visit. The joy and excitement that this woman displayed showed me again what a visit from a loved one can do.

The mitzva of visiting the ill is one of such enormous magnitude because it has the potential of bringing out the best in us as human beings.

VII

IN THE MIDST OF
BEREAVEMENT

Judaism has beautiful and sensitive customs to comfort the
bereaved. It is not my intention to examine all the feelings or
explain the laws that come into play after death. There are
already many excellent books, among them *Jewish Reflections on Death,* edited by Rabbi Jack Riemer, and *The Jewish
Way in Death and Mourning,* a superb work by Rabbi
Maurice Lamm, which I highly recommend. I would like,
though, to bring to light certain major crises that arise and
accent some beautiful customs that have evolved.

In the midst of crisis, family, patients and friends are
prone to ask the most familiar question—"why?" Understandably, most families in the midst of their crisis feel that
their suffering cannot be compared to any other's. Thus, they
feel not only grief, but deep bitterness as well. We find
throughout Jewish history the greatest leaders questioning,
but never condemning God. From Abraham pleading on
behalf of the people of Sodom and Gomorrah, to the well-
known testing of Job, and to the great Rabbi Levi Yitzchok of
Berditchev, there were those who questioned, often in a
unique way; but the fact is they did question. In my child-
hood, I was often taught that "We must never question," but
as a person who has seen suffering in my own family as well
as in others, I now strongly disagree. To question in a moment of crisis is the normal reaction of almost any mortal,
emotional human being. To be so disciplined as to accept
crisis without question is to be angelic. The Talmud (Bava

Metzia 58b) teaches, "If one is visited by suffering, afflicted with disease, or has buried children, one must not speak to him as his companions spoke to Job: "Is not thy fear of God thy confidence, and thy hope the integrity of thy ways?"

When one questions God, he is not necessarily denying His existence. He is just directing his feelings of anger and bitterness at the Almighty. It is a psychological fact that by expressing his feelings a person is better able to cope with crisis than if he were to contain them.

This story related by my father made a most powerful impression on me. The late Telzer Rosh Yeshiva (dean), Rabbi Eliyohu Meir Bloch, of blessed memory, was attending a meeting of a religious youth organization of which my father was an officer. A question was addressed to the audience, and Rabbi Bloch, the head of the seminary and a most respected figure, raised his hand to answer. My father asked, "Why is it that the Rosh Yeshiva raises his hand? Let him just speak out!"

But Rabbi Bloch replied, "As long as you realize that I am the Rosh Yeshiva, I will raise my hand, but the moment you forget, I will speak out!"

The danger sets in when we forget that it is God's judgment that we are questioning, for then we often feel that we have the right to rebel, and as a result innocent people suffer. I have watched people who have no traditional support turn to escape mechanisms such as alcohol or drugs, and while releasing their own frustrations and bitterness, cause harm to themselves or to other people. If we do want to scream out in anger, it must never be in a manner that destroys ourselves or our fellow man.

We must be aware that to be angry at God is unwarranted, and at times it is ourselves whom we have to blame. For example, when something may go wrong for a child, he may scream in a fit of anger to his parents, "It's all your fault!", when the parents were in no way responsible. Likewise, as patients, we should be honest with ourselves and know that the many so-called acts of God are perpetrated by man. We know that smoking is dangerous to our health, we know that going outside without a coat in damp weather may cause us to contract pneumonia. Heart disease, for instance, seems to be greatly influenced by lack of exercise and proper diet. The Talmud (Berachot 57b) and Maimonides (Hilchot De'ot 4) state that diet plays an important role in our health, yet we often neglect to heed these teachings. When we are afflicted with disease we cry out, "God, why do you do this to me?" Who really has been responsible?

There is a Biblical commandment—*"v'nishmartem me'od l'nafshosaichem:"* ("you shall guard your soul"—Deuteronomy 4:15). Various commentaries interpret this to mean that an individual has an obligation to guard his health. Man's psychological weakness is always to blame others rather than to face the fact that it is *he* who is often at fault.

When one cannot understand why he is suffering, he must come to the difficult realization that this misfortune is God's will, a will which is beyond our comprehension. Everyone has had their 'pekeleh', their share of problems—some more than others. We must perceive that there *is* a master plan, but we mere humans cannot have the answers to all our questions. Even if we feel that we have been righteous all our lives and are undeserving of troubles, we must believe that there is a master plan by the Creator, and, in His wisdom, the misfortunes that we experience in life have a purpose. Friends who see a patient suffering or hear of a tragedy in a particular family are especially shaken when they know that the family exemplifies the epitome of goodness. They ask themselves, "Why this person, why this family when there are so many evil ones in the world? Why do the righteous have to suffer?" The answers are not easily found, but the patients and the families who handle these crises with determination and faith can teach an eternal lesson of strength and belief to friends, families and even communities.

In the midst of bereavement, we must deal not only with our feelings, but also with the crisis itself. Death has been with us for as long as mankind has existed. Yet dying is different now. Years ago, most people died at home in a familiar environment surrounded by their families. There was a time when the body of a person who passed away at home would not be moved, and would lie covered on the floor until burial. All members of the family shared in the death experience. Death was not hidden; there was an attempt to accept it. Now, half of all deaths occur in hospitals or nursing homes, with a complete medical team in attendance.

Throughout the teachings of Judaism, whether in our daily prayers or study, we are taught that death is inevitable, that our whole life consists of preparing for the day of death. Yet, we live in a time when society seems to conceal the existence of death, with the intention of protecting us. What has really happened is that people are having greater problems today in coping with death, the final act of life. On the High Holy Days we go to the synagogue and cry out in supplication, "Mi yichyeh umi yamus—who will live and who will die?" We plead for life and acknowledge death, but we still cannot seem to cope with the latter.

Why do we fictionalize death in ways that only complicate children's lives and cause later attitudes toward death that are more fearful than they need be? I feel, in most instances, that it is important to be honest and not hide death, but to realize that His ways are above our comprehension. Our ethical treatises explain comprehension of God in an interesting analogy. Just as a painting cannot comprehend its painter or a sculpture its sculptor, so too mankind cannot begin to comprehend its Creator.

In helping the bereaved family deal with their crisis, Jewish people have had a beautiful custom for many years, and now this custom has been established in many hospitals. Services are held in which people who have experienced tragedies are brought together for prayer and companionship, enabling them to share their losses and common feelings, thereby helping them to gain strength from others who have faced similar crises.

Judaism has incorporated in its holiday prayers a beautiful and emotional service held four times a year—the "YIZKOR" service, a time of memorial. This is the one custom observed even by those who are not close to religion. They dutifully attend synagogue services and say *yizkor* for their parents or other beloved members of family. *Yizkor* is not so much for the deceased as it is for the survivors. Four times a year the child, parent, or other family member has the opportunity of coming to the synagogue before God, together with others who have suffered similar losses, to cry out and share in the memory of his beloved ones. Tears are shed readily and without shame at these services as they should be, for *yizkor* is a moment to reflect and to gain strength in dealing with a loss.

Yizkor, this beautiful memorial service, has been with us almost since the inception of prayer thousands of years ago. Only now is the recognition by our great rabbis of old of the needs of people to share in grief becoming popular. Before the *yizkor* service, it is the custom of those who have living parents to leave the services, distinguishing them from those whose parents have died. Among many German Jews however, all worshippers remain in the synagogue. Whether one remains inside or leaves the sanctuary, one is aware that *yizkor* is a special moment. Though it is a service of grieving and remembering, it is also a realization for those not saying *yizkor* that someday they too will be reciting this prayer to help absorb inevitable loss and grief. *Yizkor* is a compassionate and fulfilling moment in the traditions of Judaism.

A period of depression normally follows the death of a loved one. In the Torah we hear great men like David in Tehillim (Psalms 22:2) crying out in their isolation "*Kayli, kayli*—my God, my God, why hast Thou forsaken me?" Depression as described by Dr. Granger E. Westberg, in his excellent book *Good Grief*, "is not a feeling unique just to you or me. It's an experience that comes to all people when something or someone they love and treasure dearly is taken away from them." As Dr. Westberg beautifully describes, "what one must never forget about a depressing experience is that one day it will pass. Dark days do not last forever, the clouds are always moving, though very slowly. The person in the midst of a depression is certain, of course, that the clouds are not moving. He is convinced that this is a state in which he will remain the rest of his life. Any attempt to try to convince him otherwise is useless. However, the experience of people through the centuries has been that the dark clouds of depression *are* moving; they *do* pass. One of the most helpful things we can do for a friend at such a time is to stand by him in quiet confidence and assure him this too shall pass. He will not believe us at first, he will tell us we do not know what we are talking about. He may even ask us to leave. But he usually does not mean it. If he discovers that our concern for him is genuine, then the quiet assertion of our own confidence in God's continuing care and concern for him will assist tremendously in his recovery."

King David once asked his jeweler, "Design an article which will be both useful and ornamental." Unable to decide on anything suitable, the jeweler consulted Solomon who told him to make a ring and inscribe on it the words, "This too shall pass." When things were going well the ring would prevent a king from becoming over-confident, and when misfortune overtook him he would contemplate the inscription and realize that "this too shall pass."

After a death one may experience the natural reaction of guilt. Guilt can be the most painful companion of death. The dying patient's problems come to an end, but in a sense the family's problems continue. The family may have feelings of frustration about what they should have done or could have done (the "if" crisis), when, in reality, it did as much as it should have or could have done.

Judaism has a custom at the funeral of asking forgiveness of the deceased, if in any way we had offended him in life. This is to relieve some of the guilt feelings. If a person feels guilty for a sin he committed against someone now dead, Jewish law tells us (Shulchan Aruch, Orach Chaim 606:2) that he is to take a quorum of ten men to the graveside and ask for forgiveness. There are many ways of relieving guilt *if we acknowledge its existence.*

One of the most crucial precautions that may be taken in dealing with guilt is taking care not to lay blame on another individual; for this can cause irreversible damage. I have witnessed two incidents which aroused my concern.

CASE 1

A young man has been institutionalized for many years because of guilt attributed to him. As a teenager, he had borrowed his father's car for the evening, and while he was out, his father suffered a massive heart attack. His mother, though she called an ambulance, blamed her son for her husband's death. The teenager, who had been very close to his father became distraught, and has never recovered fully.

CASE 2

A father, while reprimanding his child, screamed out, "Do not make me sick, you will kill me yet!" Suddenly the man clutched his chest; he had suffered a fatal heart attack. This child is today institutionalized for life, unable to cope with the guilt feelings about his father's death.

In both of these instances, I was called in as a consultant. I became acutely aware that a parent must realize that when reprimanding a child, he or she is dealing with a very delicate mind. There is a world of difference between "You upset me!" and nervous, guilt-provoking irrational remarks. Parents must show a child needing discipline that though they are upset with a particular behavior, their love never ceases. After the death of a loved one or any family crisis, the need for family unity is stronger than ever. Love and affection can serve to ease the pain of one in midst of pain.

Also discussed in the book *Good Grief* is how "unresolved guilt can make one miserable for years, even to the extent of causing a variety of physical symptoms of distress." We must not be afraid or embarrassed to talk about our feelings of guilt to those who have been trained to help us when the going gets rough.

We, as the comforters, must also acknowledge that there

are certain people who can better work out their own problems, and who will call on us only when they feel they need to do so. Forcing ourselves on someone who is not ready to open up can just make a bad situation worse. But most of us do need to express our emotions and to seek comfort from our fellow man.

Guilt may be treated in various ways. I recall a process I used in dealing with an individual who had come to me after his wife died. He explained that on his wife's death-bed he had told her that he would never remarry. Now, in his early 60's, he found that he was extremely lonely, so he started dating. Yet, whenever he went out on a date he had tremendous guilt feelings, and claimed that he constantly saw his wife before him. I recommended that he travel to his wife's grave and express his feelings to her there. After accepting my advice, he returned and told me that he felt much better. He even started dating again, and his wife no longer appeared before him. He understood that his guilt feelings were aroused because his wife had been employed during their 40 years of marriage, and earned her share, which he had inherited. She did not want her earnings to be given to another woman. He therefore gave all the money that his wife had earned and saved to their children; thereafter he seemed completely free of any sense of guilt.

Psychiatrists, psychologists, social workers, nurse therapists, and many clergymen are well trained to deal with people who have burdens of guilt. One should feel free to open up to them and try to uncover the feelings that hinder one from living a normal life.

After a death some people fear contacting or speaking with the bereaved. The one who has suffered the loss will ask, "Where is everyone?" Everything becomes quiet. This feeling is especially strong in the Jewish family after the week of shiva (seven days of mourning). Having been constantly visited for an entire week, the survivors are suddenly left all alone to deal with their grief.

It is true that there comes a time when people must face tragedy alone, but there still exists a psychological vacuum after a week of attention. In a pamphlet entitled *Children Die Too*, the story is related of one family who called all their friends and begged, "Please talk to me like you used to." The bereaved family must realize that the people around them sometimes do not know how to reach out. They have feelings of awkwardness, confusion, and discomfort. People just do not know what to say, how to react, or how to relate. Often they make unintentional remarks that can cause even greater pain. Friends, when comforting a woman who had had a miscarriage, unintentionally make insensitive comments, such as "you still have healthy children; be thankful for them," or "you are still young; you will have others." These comments, though sincere, do not remove the pain of this specific loss. It is therefore appropriate for those who are grieving to somehow reach out and make their needs and desire of friendship known.

In the midst of bereavement, humanity demands that one individual must be concerned about others in need. In the biblical teaching of "Love thy neighbor as thyself" (Leviticus 19:18), we must be aware that the "I" complex is a destructive one, while the "we" complex is a constructive one. If we understand this, then the blessings of the Almighty will be imminent.

VIII

FINDING MEANS OF COMFORT

The Talmud (Eruvin 54a) states, *"Chosh b'rosho ya'asok b'Torah*—if one has a headache let him get involved in Torah."* What is meant by this suggestion? This beautiful Talmudic saying has much truth for those who are seeking comfort. The concept of having a "headache" does not necessarily mean a physical pain in the head. If an individual is lost for answers, if a person is in need of mental support, *"ya'asok b'Torah"*—the Talmud doesn't use the terminology of studying Torah, but rather getting involved in its work. One who is deeply religious can usually absorb the troubles of life. The assurance that there is someone or something to turn to can lead one a giant step forward in comforting an individual in a moment of crisis.

I recall this most powerful anecdote. Sam happened to meet his rabbi on the street one day, and told him of all the troubles he had suffered during the past year. He wound up with: "I tell you right now, rabbi, it's enough to make a man lose his religion." "Seems to me, Sam," the rabbi told him quietly, "it's enough to make a man use his religion!"

The great saint Rabbi Hirsch Michael Shapira (1840–1906) had several children who died in infancy. Yet, this never caused him to lose faith. He would say, "If not for Thy Torah to comfort me, I would be drowned in my sorrows."

When facing crisis, some people seek out religion, while others fear to approach it. An individual experiencing tragedy may doubt there is a God who is listening. Or he might

say, "Why bother to pray?" These philosophical and psychological confusions paralyze the natural instincts to appeal to
a Higher Power. However, in a moment of reconsideration,
these confusions may be solved.

When my child was ill, I wondered for a moment, "Where
do I turn?" And then the obvious dawned on me. I walked
into my synagogue and opened the Holy Ark. I cried and
pleaded. I honestly felt that Someone was there listening.
Someone with whom to talk. To believe and have faith, even
in a moment of grave crisis, is to be comforted as well.

Prayer is talking to God. To some it is instinctive. They
pray automatically without having to think about it. For
others, problems arise when they forget to think about it.

When facing crisis, many go to synagogues or other houses
of worship and offer prayers in behalf of the ill. Patients
often ask me to pray for them. I, of course, assure them that I
will, but I have always told these patients, "Do not think for
one moment that my offering prayers may be greater than
you yourself praying. Being a rabbi does not make me any
greater in the eyes of God than you, a layman."

There is a Jewish custom that when a person is gravely ill,
psalms are said and a special invocation is recited in the
synagogue. Personally, I have witnessed the power of prayer
warding off death numerous times.

I have read articles written by individuals who were never
actively religious at the time of a beloved one's death, but
they went to the synagogue to say the *Kaddish* prayer or to
try to find a sense of comfort in its surroundings. They then
suddenly felt themselves becoming more involved in religious experiences. In all sincerity, let us ask ourselves, might
not these challenges and crises that occur in life be God's
way of bringing us closer to Him?

As I have repeatedly stated, God's ways can never be explained. In the Torah (Exodus 33:23), Moses asked to see
God face to face, but the Almighty answered him, "My face
you cannot see, but my back shall be shown to you." Commentaries explain that sometimes we cannot understand
why certain things happen; we are troubled and bitter, and

we demand at that moment to understand why. However, when we look back later, perhaps then we can begin to understand why certain things in our lives happened. There is a moving story of a man who was mourning the loss of his beloved wife. While walking on the beach, in his anguish he cried out to the Almighty, "You promised to walk along side me in times of trouble but when I look down I only see one set of footprints." There was silence and then a voice lovingly called out, "My dear child, what seems to be one pair of footprints is not really you walking alone. It is me carrying you."

I have had a child who was born ill, and had a child who died; though I cried bitterly and I questioned, today I honestly believe that my crises caused other individuals to come closer to God. There was a reawakening of community prayer; there was a recommitment to the giving of charity. It is unfortunate but true that crisis often awakens the dormant.

It is written in the Torah (Exodus 19:16) that the Ten Commandments were given in an atmosphere of *Kolos Uvrokim:* with loud thunderous noises, not in the midst of a calm and sunny day. Why? Can it be because the Almighty saw that it takes a shock reaction for man to understand that life hungers for action and acceptance of responsibilities?

I have often heard members of certain religious denominations saying that they do not believe in after-life. To them I firmly ask, "How then, do you find comfort or comfort someone who is suffering amongst you? If your teachings are that there is no life after death, be it spiritual or physical, then what explanation is there for our being? Surely it cannot be just an animalistic existence. There must be, and is more to the purpose and gift of life."

In Maurice Lamm's outstanding work entitled *The Jewish Way in Death and Mourning* (Jonathan David Publishers, New York, pages 222–224), he retells a beautiful parable. "An imaginative and telling analogy that conveys the hope and confidence in the after-life, even though this hope must be refracted through the prism of death, is the tale of twins awaiting birth in the mother's womb. It was created by a contemporary Israeli rabbi, the late Y. M. Tuckachinsky.

Imagine twins growing peacefully in the warmth of the womb. Their mouths are closed, and they are being fed via the navel. Their lives are serene. The whole world, to these brothers, is the interior of the womb. Who could conceive anything larger, better, more comfortable? They begin to wonder: "We are getting lower and lower. Surely if this continues, we will exit one day. What will happen after we exit?"

Now the first infant is a believer. He is heir to a religious tradition which tells him that there will be a "new life" after this wet and warm existence of the womb. A strange belief, seemingly without foundation, but one to which he holds fast. The second infant is a thorough-going skeptic. Mere stories do not deceive him. He believes only in that which can be demonstrated. He is enlightened, and tolerates no idle conjecture. What is not within one's experience can have no basis in one's imagination.

Says the faithful brother: "After our 'death' here, there will be a new great world. We will eat through the mouth! We will see great distances, and we will hear through the ears on the sides of our heads. Why, our feet will be straightened! And our heads—up and free, rather than down and boxed in."

Replies the skeptic: "Nonsense. You're straining your imagination again. There is no foundation for this belief. It is only your survival instinct, an elaborate defense mechanism, a historically-conditioned subterfuge. You are looking for something to calm your fear of 'death.' There is only this world. There is no world-to-come!"

"Well then," askes the first, "what do you say it will be like?"

The second brother snappily replies with all the assurance of the slightly knowledgeable: "We will go with a bang. Our world will collapse and we will sink into oblivion. No more. Nothing. Black void. An end to consciousness. Forgotten.

This may not be a comforting thought, but it is a logical one."

Suddenly the water inside the womb bursts. The womb convulses. Upheaval. Turmoil. Writhing. Everything lets loose. Then a mysterious pounding—a crushing, staccato pounding. Faster, faster, lower, lower.

The believing brother exits. Tearing himself from the womb, he falls outward. The second brother shrieks—startled by the "accident" which has befallen his brother. He bewails and bemoans the tragedy—the death of a perfectly fine fellow. Why? Why? Why didn't he take better care? Why did he fall into that terrible abyss?

As he thus laments, he hears a head-splitting cry, and a great tumult from the black abyss, and he trembles: "Oh my! What a horrible end! As I predicted!"

Meanwhile as the skeptic brother mourns, his "dead" brother has been born into the "new" world. The head-splitting cry is a sign of health and vigor, and the tumult is really a chorus of *mazel tovs* sounded by the waiting family thanking God for the birth of a healthy son.

Indeed, in the words of a contemporary thinker, man comes from the darkness of the "not yet," and proceeds to the darkness of "no more." While it is difficult to imagine the "not yet" it is more difficult to picture the "no more."

As we separate and "die" from the womb, only to be born to life, so we separate and die from our world, only to be reborn to life eternal. The exit from the womb is the birth of the body. The exit from the body is the birth of the soul. As the womb requires a gestation period of nine months, the world requires a residence of 70 or 80 years. As the womb is *prozdor*, an anteroom preparatory to life, so our present existence is a prozdor to the world beyond.

In counseling individuals who are attempting to cope with either problems of illness or other crisis, I have, at times, been able to offer some understanding. In many families I receive a response that evokes the basic message of this book—"Rabbi, I can understand what you are saying and it would comfort if one is religious, but what do you do about the one that is not?" It is a fact that a religious person, no matter how his religion is defined, can cope much better with crisis situations, while a person without religion will never find true comfort.

I have chosen to include in this book an article written by a woman who shares her feelings and experiences as she and her family lived through her husband's critical illness. I too witnessed this miracle and choose to share it with you, the reader, for it epitomizes the degree of faith and love.

A JEWISH RESPONSE TO CRISIS

Channukah was approaching, and my eight year old daughter excitedly waved her hand, wanting to answer her Hebrew teacher's question, "Since the days of the miracle of the oil, have any modern day miracles occurred?" Lisa was called on and answered with pride and awe, "My Daddy is a miracle. He was very sick and in a coma, but God brought him back to us."

This story is about that miracle, but it is also about much more. It is about the support and concern Jews show one another in times of crisis. It is about the faith and strength Judaism provides for those who seek it. Finally, it is about a man, my husband, who awoke from an encounter with death and turned it into an affirmation of life.

This all began two and one half years ago when my husband Yale, a 37 year old accountant, developed flu-like symptoms which rapidly intensified with fevers of 105°. After examining him, the doctor felt it was a virus that "was going around," and he monitored the situation daily. Finally, after several days, the fever subsided, and Yale prepared to return to work. He felt quite weak, and like any protective wife, I urged him to stay home; like any ambitious husband, he believed he had to get back to work and was about to do so when he suddenly felt faint, collapsed on the bed, cried out that he couldn't see me, and went into convulsions. I called the paramedics who conveyed him to the hospital where he was admitted. Though at first dehydration from the high fever seemed a possible explanation since his sight had returned, this diagnosis faded as the day progressed since further seizures occurred, and then his sight and hearing started to waver again. That evening, a spinal tap and other tests were done and the verdict was clear—viral encephalitis, an inflammation of the brain. It was a word I was only vaguely familiar with then, but has become an integral part of our lives ever since. As Yale's brother and I received the news, we were stunned but not hopeless, because we were told as long as Yale maintained consciousness, the virus just had to run its course, and perhaps this nightmare might conclude with minimal danger. In the week that followed, Yale's sight and hearing continued to fade in and out, and his seizures continued. My heart broke as I imagined the agony and pain he must be suffering, but he never complained. Only later did I learn that even today, he has no memory of this period. Our hopes ebbed and waned with each day as we looked for signs of improvement, until one day, a week later, our neurologist came to us with the word that jolts a family into total despair—COMA. Yale was now in a comatose state from which he would probably never emerge. If he did survive, most likely his sight would never be restored, extensive brain damage seemed unavoidable, and many other equally horrifying possibilities presented themselves.

What does one do as a 33 year old mother of two daughters, aged 3 and 6, when confronted with such doom?

What I did first was to find guidance and comfort from my Jewish "network" of clergymen and laymen alike. Our rabbi was summoned when we received news of Yale's comatose state, and he literally "picked up the pieces of my emotional being." With warmth and wisdom, he convinced me it was impossible to absorb and confront the whole picture at once, and that I must just cope moment by moment until we could perceive a clearer picture later on. In the weeks to follow, I found relevance and comfort in his practical yet inspiring guidance. To this day, I feel a deep personal bond with him.

I discovered a different kind of inspiration from another

rabbi whose support was equally invaluable. He was a rabbi whom Yale and I had known for several years through our local Chabad house. Upon initially hearing the news of Yale's illness, he came each day to help Yale lay *tefillin* until he lapsed into a coma. He also consulted the Lubavitch Rebbe who felt strongly that Yale's *tefillin* be examined to see if they were kosher; upon discovering they were not, he encouraged me to purchase new ones, and gave me assurance that Yale would successfully survive this ordeal. This decisive message of hope amidst oppressive gloom revitalized my spirits, although it was viewed with some skepticism by many around me. I purchased the *tefillin*, and to this day, Yale cherishes them and uses them faithfully. Our local Lubavitch Rabbi and his wife became my "extended family." They were with me constantly in the hospital and opened their home to me for Shabbat, since they lived near the hospital. I truly believe my pain was their pain and, in the end, my joy was their joy. I will never forget their devotion and love.

The word of Yale's illness spread rapidly throughout the Jewish community, and rabbis whom I didn't even know extended their support, concern and prayers. The lay community as well demonstrated its sense of unity. They heard that a young Jewish husband and father was battling for his life, and this seemed to produce a feeling of mutual sorrow and alarm which touched many. Our congregation, especially, pulled together and set up informal networks so that Yale's condition was monitored by all. I recall hearing that the day he came out of the coma, one congregant spotted another in a neighborhood supermarket parking lot and, with tears in her eyes, ran up to her saying, "Did you hear? Yale Freiman is out of the coma!" The rabbi, from his pulpit, also informed the congregation of Yale's status so that when he finally began to recover, an atmosphere of relief and gladness permeated the synagogue. Our *chavurah*, however, best exemplified this bond between fellow Jews. We had been members of this study/social group of ten couples for several years when Yale became ill. Upon learning of Yale's plight, they arranged a special meeting where one of the members, a physician, explained all the implications of encephalitis, and they then deliberated over how they might best assist us. Some took our children on outings, others brought us groceries, some who kept kosher prepared meals, and still others drove me to the hospital. They became a source of practical assistance and emotional sustenance.

Finally, our family and friends literally surrounded us with love and support so that I was rarely ever alone in that foreboding place called "the intensive care waiting room." I've often thought that this room envelopes the depths of human tragedy as one waits to hear news of life and death. As I waited so many hours for just that kind of news, invariably there were aunts, uncles, cousins, and dear friends who had the fortitude and compassion to wait and hope and pray with me there. Under those circumstances it is impossible to feel abandoned and hopeless.

However, in the midst of such a crisis, outside support can only provide a portion of the sustenance one needs. The rest must come from within, from a source I call faith. Never before had I felt such a deep spiritual bond with God as I did during those weeks of uncertainty. Our rabbi had given me a small pamphlet of prayers called "Fountain of Life," and it became my means of communication with God. Especially at night, when I lay in bed, afraid to face the anxieties and uncertainties of the morrow, I reached for that booklet, and the words therein literally sustained me and enabled me to overcome my fears and find rest and reassurance. One in particular captured my mood and needs:

God of our life, there are days when our burdens overwhelm us, when the road ahead seems dreary, when the skies are grey and threatening. On such days our lives have no music, our hearts are lonely and our spirits are robbed of courage. Flood our path with light, we beseech You; direct our vision to promising skies; attune our hearts to the uplifting music of life. Grant us the awareness of true comradeship with others, to sustain us, and so quicken our spirits that we may be able to encourage those who journey with us on the road of life to dedicate themselves to your honor and glory.

I was not the only one who turned to prayer in our time of crisis and drew strength from it. Yale's mother recited *tehillim* (psalms) at home and in the hospital morning and night. I know that all our loved ones, in their own ways, turned to God to ask for His intervention and healing. In all our cards and letters, phone calls, and conversations, people told us they were praying. Those prayers spanned the coasts of this country, and a few made their way to the Wall in Jerusalem. However, no prayers were more touching or sincere than those of our children. Each night, before going to bed, they gave *tzedakah* (charity) and then in their own words, asked God's blessings for their Dad. I truly believe that of all the prayers, those must have had the most profound impact.

This reliance on faith and prayer has a marvelous component—strength! I am convinced God enabled our family to discover and utilize strength we could never have imagined. He gave me the capacity to hold my elder daughter in my arms and gently explain to her that her Daddy might never get well, but we would still be a family and love one another just the same. God gave her the courage to want to see Yale in Intensive Care, despite her fears in doing so, so she could perhaps have a last chance to tell him she loved him. God instilled in our family the strength to sit and rationally debate the advisability of initiating life support systems, if the situation arose. Finally, He invoked in me a determination to "get through to Yale", even if it meant sitting for hours and hours, speaking words of support and encouragement without any tangible signs of response. All in all, God imbued within us the strength to just cope with each day, always mindful of the fact that it could be the fatal last one. In the words of Isaiah 40:29, 31, "He gives vigor to the weary, new strength to the exhausted. Those who hope in the Lord will gain new strength."

However, the person who was infused with the greatest strength was Yale himself. When he miraculously awoke from the coma after fifteen days, he was like an alien. Everything appeared chaotic and confusing. He couldn't remember what had precipitated his being in a hospital. His memory about other aspects of his life were severely limited. He had to begin to learn and develop much the way a baby does, but with the frustration of knowing he was an adult. Embarking on a defined program of physical and occupational therapy, he began to learn to walk, talk, dress himself, and slowly master such simple tasks as dialing a telephone or writing his name. The amazing part was that he tackled each task with a determination that left the therapists breathless. He really believed God had given him a second chance at life, and he couldn't wait to begin living it. Even when he came home, he viewed our children, family, friends and career as gifts never to be taken for granted again.

I began this article with the word "miracle", and I will end it the same way. It is a miracle, because a person in the throes of death has been restored, virtually unmarred. It is a miracle, because a family has been made whole again, and because we have all been given an opportunity to view life from a different perspective. We no longer feel such crises only happen to others. We don't believe health is a given, a certainty rather than a gift. We now feel, stronger than ever, that Judaism is a priceless resource, providing a sense of community, faith, strength, and hope. A deeper observance of the Sabbath and holidays has evolved from this renewal, and it has added joy and beauty to our lives. As I end this article, Yale has just celebrated his 40th birthday. Though he may "be over the hill" to some, we are thrilled he was able to make the journey.

The book of Psalms (145:18) states that God is near to those who call upon Him faithfully. Only the individual himself, family or patient in the midst of crisis, can interpret faithfulness. When seeking comfort, let us turn to the Creator of all to give us the strength to live through our moments of crisis.

CONCLUSION

I realize that there are those who will continue to grieve after reading this book. Reading all the books printed cannot bring back a loved one or answer unanswerable questions. We must recognize that if we were born with all the education we needed, then what reason would there be for schooling, what challenge would there be in life? For life to mean something, moments of challenge must exist. Unfortunately, some moments will be sad ones, but they will exist until the fulfillment of the prophecy "when mankind will no longer have reason to suffer" (Isaiah 25:8).

During the Days of Awe, we make an addition into our prayers, asking God to *remember us for life, the King who wants life, inscribe us in the Book of Life.* I ask the question, if we are asking God to remember us for life, why do we need to request from Him that He write this down as well? God is not man, that we must have him sign and seal a commitment that he makes. If God remembers us for life, is that not enough? I would like to interpret that the purpose of the added request to write us in the Book of Life is to restrain the angel of death. For, once it is written that the gift of life has been granted, even the angel of death has no power over this decree. While God most surely wants man to live and will remember us for life, we must still pray that that evil angel of death be subdued and eventually destroyed.

The prophecy of Isaiah will become a reality when, "He will swallow up death forever; and the Lord God will wipe away tears from off all faces; and the reproach of His people will He take away from off all the earth."

Judaism believes in the concept of purgatory, a purification process before we enter the next world. Perhaps purgatory also exists in this life as well, and thus a person's suffering, child or adult, serves as a cleansing or purifying process preparing him to enter directly into the world of eternal reward.

There is so much more that can be written but I have made every attempt to keep this book concise and not to overburden the reader. This book is only a beginning; your clergyman can work with you to reach the end.

In closing I share the thought quoted by the renowned psychiatrist and philosopher, Dr. Viktor Frankl, in his work, *Man's Search for Meaning*, "He who has a *why* to live for, can bear with almost any *how*". I pray that all of us who have suffered through illness and crisis can find that "why" and realize that the Jewish way of coping is the acceptance that in every facet of living, God TAKES, but God GIVES, BLESSED BE HIS NAME FOREVER AND EVER.

BIBLIOGRAPHY

Babylonian Talmud. New York (S. Goldman—Otzar Haseforim Inc.), 1961.

Bachya, Ibn Paqudda. *Duties of the Heart*, English translation by Moses Hyamson, New York (Feldheim Publishers), 1970.

Birnbaum, Philip. *High Holiday Prayer Book*. New York (Hebrew Publishing Co.), 1951.

Blaine, Graham B. Jr., "Youth, Religion, and the New Morality" *Journal of Religion and Health*—5. (1966) 7–16.

Bokser, Benzion (Translator). *Abraham Isaac Kook*. New York (Paulist Press), 1978.

Bunim, Irving M. *Ethics from Sinai*. New York (Philip Feldheim Inc.— 3 volumes), 1964.

Cousins, Norman. *Anatomy of an Illness*. New York (Bantam Books), 1979.

Davidson, Glen W. *Living with Dying*. Minneapolis, Minn. (Augsburg Publishing), 1975.

Dresner, Samuel H. "The Deaths of the Hasidic Masters (From the *Histalkut Hanefesh*) in *Jewish Reflections on Death*, edited Jack Riemer. New York (Schocken Books), 1974. 24–30.

Frankel, Rabbi I. *Men of Distinction*. Tel Aviv, Israel (Sinai Publishing), 1967.

Frankl, Viktor E. *Man's Search for Meaning*. New York (Washington Square Press), 1963.

Grollman, Earl A. (editor). *Rabbinical Counseling*. New York (Bloch Publishing Co.), 1966.

The Holy Scriptures (translation). Philadelphia, Pa. (Jewish Publication Society of America), 1917.

Jackson, Basil. "Psychology, Psychiatry & the Pastor", (Part I), *Bibliotheca Sacra*, Dallas, Texas (Dallas Theological Seminary), 1975 p. 3–15.

Jakobovits, Immanuel. *Jewish Medical Ethics*. New York (Bloch Publishing Co.), 1959.

Johnson, Joy & Johnson, S.M. (Pamphlet). *Children Die Too*. Omaha, Nebraska (Centering Corporation), 1978.

Johnson, Joy & Johnson, S.M. (Pamphlet). *Miscarriage*. Omaha, Nebraska (Centering Corporation), 1983.

Jung, Carl. *Modern Man in Search of a Soul*. New York (Harcourt, Brace, Inc.), 1933.

Jung, Carl. "The Interpretation of Visions", *Analytical Psychology*. New York (1962), 107–157.

Kaplan, Aryeh. *If You Were God*. New York (National Conference of Synagogue Youth), 1983.

Kidorf, Irwin, W. "The Shiva: a form of group psychotherapy." *Journal of Religion and Health*—5. (1966), 43–46.

Koheleth Rabba in *Midrash Rabba* on *The Five Books of the Torah and the Five Scrolls*. New York (Ktav Publishing House, Inc.), No date given.

Kubler-Ross, Elisabeth. *On Death and Dying*. New York (Macmillan Publishing Co.), 1969.

Kubler-Ross, Elisabeth. *Questions and Answers on Death and Dying*. New York (Macmillan Publishing Co.), 1974.

Kubler-Ross, Elisabeth. *Death the Final Stage of Growth*. Englewood Cliff, New Jersey (Prentice Hall Inc.), 1975.

Kupfer, Fern. *Before and After Zachyria*. New York (Delacorte Press), 1971.

Kushner, Harold S. *When Bad Things Happen to Good People*. New York (Avon Books), 1981.

LaHaye, Tim. *How to Win Over Depression*. Grand Rapids, Mich. (Zondervan Publishing House), 1974.

Lamm, Maurice. *The Jewish Way in Death and Mourning*. New York (Jonathan David Publishing), 1969.

Levine, Joseph. "Bikkur Cholim: A Clinical Perspective", *Journal of Reform Judaism*—25 (1979) 25–34.

Luzzatto, Moshe Chaim. *Mesilat Yeshorim*. (The Path of the Just.) New York (Feldheim), 1966.

Maimonides, Moses. Mishneh Torah: Hilchot Rotzeach U'Shmiras Hanefesh (Laws of Homicide and Life Preservation), New York (Freidman Publishing), 1963.

Mserve, Harry C. "Man's Ministry to Man", *Journal of Religion and Health*—5, (1966) 61–76.

Midrash Mishle, edited S. Buber, Wilna, 1893.

Midrash Yalkut Shimoni, edited Rabeinu Shimon, Jerusalem, Israel, 1959.

Murray, Mrs. Max A. "Needs of Parents of Mentally Retarded Children", *American Journal of Mental Deficiency*—63, (1959) 1078–1088.

Myerhoff, Barbara. *Number Our Days*. New York (E. P. Dutton), 1979.

Neuwin, Henri J. M. & Gaffney, Walter J. *Aging the Fulfillment of Life*. Garden City, New York (Image Books), 1976.

Niklas, Gerald R. and Stafanics, Charlotte. *Ministry to the Sick*, New York (Alba House), 1982.

Pliskin, Zelig. *Gateway to Happiness*. Monsey, New York (Jewish Learning Exchange), 1983.

Potok, Chaim. *My Name is Asher Lev*. New York (Alfred K. Knopf), 1972.

Powell, John. *Fully Human Fully Alive*. Niles, Ill. (Argus Communications), 1976.

Rosner, Fred. *Modern Medicine and Jewish Law*. New York (Bloch Publishing for Yeshiva University Press), 1972.

Rosner, Fred & Bleich, J. David. *Jewish Bioethics*. New York (Sanhedrin Press), 1979.

Sabom, Michael B. *Recollections of Death: A Medical Investigation*. New York (Harper & Row Publishers), 1982.

Sandler, Nat H. "Attitudes of Ministers toward Psychiatry", *Journal of Religion and Health*—5. (1966) 47–60.

Sanford, John A. *Healing and Wholeness*. New York (Paulist Press), 1977.

Saunders, Cicely. *Care of the Dying*. London (Macmillan & Co. Ltd.), 1960.

Schiff, Harriet S. *The Bereaved Parent*. New York (Crown Publishers Inc.), 1977.

Sharpe, William D. *Medicine and the Ministry*. New York (Appleton-Century), 1966.

Shulchan Aruch: Yoreh Deah. New York (Otzar Halacha), 1960.

Simon, Sidney. *Feeling, Caring, Teaching*. Niles, Ill. (Argus Communications), 1976.

Spero, Moshe. *Judaism and Psychology: Halachic Perspectives*. New York (Ktav/Yeshiva University Press), 1980.

Tendler, Moshe B. *Medical Ethics*. New York (Federation of Jewish Philanthropies), 1975.

Westberg, Granger E. *Good Grief*. Philadelphia, Pa. (Fortress Press), 1962, 1971.

Winkler, Gershon. *The Soul of the Matter*. New York (Judaica Press), 1984.

Wolff, Pierre. *May I Hate God?*. New York (Paulist Press), 1979.